Black American Poets Between Worlds, 1940–1960

KNOXVILLE

TENNESSEE STUDIES IN LITERATURE VOLUME 30

Black American Poets Between Worlds, 1940–1960

Edited by R. Baxter Miller

THE UNIVERSITY OF TENNESSEE PRESS

Copyright © 1986 by The University of Tennessee Press / Knoxville. All Rights Reserved. Manufactured in the United States of America. First Edition.

Publication of this book has been aided by a grant from The Better English Fund, established by John C. Hodges at The University of Tennessee, Knoxville.

"Tennessee Studies in Literature," a distinguished series sponsored by the Department of English at The University of Tennessee, Knoxville, began publication in 1956. Beginning in 1984, with Volume 27, TSL evolved from a series of annual volumes of miscellaneous essays to a series of occasional volumes, each one dealing with a specific theme, period, or genre, for which the editor of that volume has invited contributions from leading scholars in the field.

The paper used in this book meets the minimum requirements of the American National Standard for Permanence of Paper for Printed Library Materials, Z39.48-1984. Binding materials have been chosen for durability.

∞ ™

Library of Congress Cataloging-in-Publication Data

Main entry under title:

Black American poets between worlds, 1940–1960.

(Tennessee studies in literature ; v. 30)
Includes index.
1. American poetry — Afro-American authors — History and criticism — Addresses, essays, lectures.
2. American poetry — 20th century — History and criticism — Addresses, essays, lectures. 3. Afro-Americans in literature — Addresses, essays, lectures. I. Miller, R. Baxter. II. Series.
PS153.N5B535 1986   811'.5'09896073   85-22644
ISBN 0-87049-499-6 (alk. paper)

Editorial Board

Allison R. Ensor
Thomas J. Heffernan
B.J. Leggett
Norman Sanders
Jon Manchip White

Inquiries concerning this series should be addressed to the Editorial Board, *Tennessee Studies in Literature,* Department of English, The University of Tennessee, Knoxville, Tennessee 37996-0430. Those desiring to purchase additional copies of this issue or copies of back issues should address The University of Tennessee Press, 293 Communications Building, Knoxville, Tennessee 37996-0325.

For George E. Kent, 1920–1982

who left behind him "monuments of unaging intellect" . . .

Beyond steps that occur and close,
your steps are echo-makers.
You can never be forgotten.

— Gwendolyn Brooks

Reclaim now, now renew the vision of
a human world where godliness
is possible and man
is neither gook nigger honkey wop nor kike

but man

   permitted to be man.

   — ROBERT HAYDEN

Contents

R. Baxter Miller

Preface

This book presents, for the first time, scholarly and critical appraisals of poetry by Black American writers who established reputations between 1940 and 1960. These literary careers began to flower during the well-known Harlem Renaissance of the 1920s, a period of militant integration, and continued through the Black Arts Movement of the 1960s, a decade of militant separatism. Born about the time of World War I, the poets, except for Melvin B. Tolson, were first children of the Renaissance, then young adults during World War II, and finally middle-aged artists during the Korean conflict. As fully blossomed voices in the Civil Rights Movement (1960–1975), the poets have now maintained intellectual and literary influence in the current time of the New Conservatism and the Moral Majority. After their experience with the stereotypical belief in Black exoticism during the twenties and with various wars from the forties through the sixties, the poets have implicitly balanced mimetic and apocalyptic theories of literature. In Freudian terms these poets play the id against the superego, and in Derridean terms they aesthetically reconstruct ethical and phenomenological values. Through ballad, sonnet, and free verse, they are the poets of memory, protest, tradition, and cultural celebration.

The poets employ a variety of technical skills, including the romantic rhetoric, the dramatic situation, and the manipulation of narrative viewpoint; the authors fuse the artistic sensibility with the aesthetic object and the re-creation of modern consciousness.[1] Where modern poetry in the mainstream moves toward anti-heroism and disorder as well as toward suicide, Black poetry — a genre in its own right — asserts a bolder heroism.[2] Through the verses, the humanist tradition still resists defeat. Here the structures are complex and irreducible; the postures are ironic, sarcastic, humorous, distant, and sympathetic. When the middle generation of Black poets resists any attempts to narrow humane meaning, their verses fuse conscience and craft.

The essays in this book make an original contribution to literary scholarship in the United States, particularly as regards Afro-American poetry. Although a volume or two now recounts the life and work of Melvin B. Tolson, and although Robert Hayden has received consistent attention in scholarly journals since 1980,[3] assessments of poetry by Dudley Randall and Margaret Danner are absent. Lately the poetry of Margaret Walker (Alexander) has earned an article or two, but the student searches in vain for the sustained study that Walker's work merits. While Gwendolyn Brooks has been the focus of a Twayne study and a critical biography, perceptive attention to her writing remains insufficient. In my opinion Brooks ranks among the five or ten most talented poets writing English in the twentieth century, and one expects to see more serious criticism. The essayists writing for this volume rectify this scholarly neglect and encourage the reconsideration, indeed the elevation, of the poets they consider, writers whose efforts already rank among the high achievement in Black American literary history.

The book covers the work of six poets and suggests theoretical assumptions for reading their work in broad terms. For Tolson and Walker, as well as for Brooks since 1967, the volume implies the interplay between speech and writing. The essays touch upon the private worlds of Dudley Randall and Margaret Danner, and the articles also indicate the strong attraction to epic poetry on the part of Tolson, Hayden, Walker, and Brooks. Whether read as textual study, or as formal analysis, the book may lead the reader indirectly to an appreciation for the way these poets create Judaeo-Christian and folk codes.

Whatever their genres or sources, the poets merit acclaim for their skilled use of figurative language. While no real "whirlwind" probably occurred historically between 1940 and 1960, as at least one literary historian has implied, the imagery of disheveled air embodies the metaphorical power and complex symbolism of the poets discussed. When the narrator in Brooks' "The Second Sermon on the Warpland" addresses some younger listeners, she urges them to face the storm of human life directly.

But Dudley Randall's speaker presents a more subtle view of the whirlwind in "Profile on the Pillow." Indeed, Randall's own "Ballad of Birmingham" and Margaret Danner's "Slave and the Iron Lace," which are more oblique poems, share the coded meaning: in the decade of riot, upheaval, and martyrdom — the 1960s — the poets of the middle generation have sought to reorient themselves to the ideals of beauty, nobility, and love, the best legacy from the Harlem Renaissance; yet they have committed themselves to their children, to the future of Black America, and to the most pragmatic prospects for a humane world. Although literary historians write discursively about the past, poets write both metaphorically and diachronically about the future. So often the scholar must read the poets on their own terms.

Limited by space, the coverage of the poets' work in this book is not exhaustive. While the consideration of other poets of the generation, including Frank Marshall Davis, Waring Cuney, and Owen Dodson, would have been a valuable addition, this volume emphasizes the work of writers who are frequently taught in colleges and universities. Priority is given to critical evaluation rather than literary history, an equally valuable enterprise. While literary history attempts to read literature against the pattern of social causality, literary criticism seeks to extrapolate patterns from literary history and human consciousness. Fortunately, the distinction is not absolute, and, from Professor Russell's essay at the beginning of the volume to mine at the close, every contributor considers the principles of literary form and literary history. Russell, Shaw, and Fetrow combine psychological and social method in the critical assessment. Indebted to all of the other authors, I myself explore the bond between form and myth.

Acknowledgments are appropriate to many colleagues. Particular gratitude goes to Allison R. Ensor and Norman J. Sanders, who encouraged and helped shape the project. I thank Carol Orr, director of the press, who has constantly encouraged me to get a good manuscript into production soon. I also thank the trustees of the Better English Fund established by John C. Hodges and administered by the Department of English at the University of Tennessee, Knoxville, for the financial support to provide honoraria for the contributors to this volume. Finally, I thank Jessica, my wife, and Akin, my eight-year-old son, who eventually decided not to banish me from the family, despite my purchase of an IBM computer to expedite manuscript preparation.

NOTES

1. See Arthur P. Davis, "Toward the Mainstream (1940–1960)," in *From the Dark Tower: Afro-American Writers 1900–1960* (Washington, D.C.: Howard Univ. Press, 1974), 137–46; Woodie King, Jr., ed., *The Forerunners: Black Poets in America* (Washington, D.C.: Howard Univ. Press, 1981), ix. Richard Barksdale and Keneth Kinnamon, *Black Writers of America: A Comprehensive Anthology* (New York: Macmillan, 1972), 479, 655; Arthur P. Davis and Saunders Redding, eds., *Cavalcade: Negro American Writing from 1760 to the Present* (New York: Houghton Mifflin, 1971), 235.

2. See M.L. Rosenthal, *The New Poets* (London: Oxford Univ. Press, 1967), 1–20.

3. See Mariann Russell, "Ghetto Laughter: A Note on Tolson's Style," *Obsidian: Black Literature in Review*, 5, Nos. 1 & 2 (Spring/Summer 1979), 7–16; Mariann Russell, *Melvin B. Tolson's Harlem Gallery: A Literary Analysis* (Columbia: Univ. of Missouri Press, 1980); Robert M. Farnsworth, "What Can A Poet Do? Langston Hughes and M.B. Tolson," *New Letters*, 48 (1981–82), 19–29; Fred M. Fetrow, "'Middle Passage': Robert Hayden's Anti-Epic," *CLA Journal*, 22 (1978/79), 304–18; Vilma Raskin Potter, "A Remembrance for Robert Hayden, 1913–1980," *MELUS*, 8, No. 1 (Spring 1981), 51–55; William H. Hansell, "The Spiritual Unity of Robert Hayden's *Angle of Ascent*," *Black American Literature Forum*, 13, no. 1 (Spring 1979), 24–31; Pantheolla Williams, "A Critical Analysis of the Poetry of Robert Hayden Through the Middle Years," *DAI*, 41 (1980), 1835A; Phanuel Egejuru and Robert Eliot Fox, "An Interview with Margaret Walker," *Callaloo* (May 1979), 19–35.

Mariann B. Russell

Evolution of Style in the Poetry of Melvin B. Tolson

The consideration of Melvin Tolson's evolving style concerns the maturation of his thought. Here I concentrate on his epic form and his developing perspective. I shall first generalize about his world-view and then trace the development of the hero figure, for both processes set into relief the stylistic growth. The examination includes less the discussion of metrics and figurative language than the concern for poetics in the deepest sense.

Tolson writes: "A great preacher is a great artist. Words are his tubes of paint. Verse, his brush."[1] These sentences go far to explain the poetics of the speaker. He does not belong to that stream of Anglo-American poetry which is purely lyric, expressing directly and mellifluously the poet's own emotions. He concerns himself, on the contrary, with social issues as the barebones of life. His style comes closer to oratorical rhetoric than to song, and his poem is generally public rather than confessional.

The son of a "fighting preacher" — "I used to watch my Dad in the pulpit and feel proud . . ."[2] — Tolson was himself a great speaker and debate coach as well as a director of theater. Concerned with the underdog in general and with the Black underdog in particular, he saw words as weapons in the war against social ills. Closely linked to the Afro-American oral tradition and the personal commitment to fighting injustice, he shaped a Christo-Marxist worldview.[3] As in the poetry of others during the thirties, his lyric encompassed a social, metaphysical, and communal burden.

Over the years he had four books of poetry published. The first, written about 1934, was brought out posthumously. *A Gallery of Harlem Portraits*,[4] as it was called, contained verses about Harlemites. His next book was *Rendezvous with America* (1944),[5] a collection somewhat influenced by World War II; his third volume, *Libretto for the Republic of Liberia* (1953),[6] was written after he had been chosen the poet-laureate of the country so named. In "academic" style the booklength ode celebrates the African nation. His final volume, *Harlem Gallery* (1965),[7] was another booklength ode, intended as the beginning of an epic about the American Black.

Before undertaking any discussion of the first book, it would be helpful to outline Tolson's cultural theory. His poetry begins with his life experience, which he mulls over, talks over, and subsumes into his phenomenally eclectic reading. Then he transmutes the whole into verse. For the talented and intellectually probing college professor in the Southwest and West from 1923 to 1965, racial discrimination and prejudice were abiding concerns. A Jim Crow existence provoked direct protest and probing into human nature. The Marxist interpretation became a focal point of his thought.[8]

Tolson's epic intention persists in varying forms. In a world that is class-divided and economically determined, the exploited masses become crucial. The underdog, the despised, the poor appear heroic now and foreshadow even greater heroism after the establishment of a new society. Tolson, sometimes ironically, celebrates the human potential embodied in the voiceless majority of the underprivileged.

The masses, in their human potential, become an abstract ideal, a generic hero. But Tolson finds individual nations such as America and Liberia heroic in the present promise and in the future apocalypse. Individual characters who are heroic include persons like Crispus Attucks and Paul Bunyan as well as the poet-prophet, the "ape of God." In one way or another, such various heroes inform his epics.

But Tolson is not merely an epic poet looking for an epic hero. His perspective encourages the epic search, since he proposes the great man theory of history. In his newspaper columns he asserts that geniuses improve humanity's lot. He cites poets, prophets, and scholars as specific types through whose efforts humankind comes to understand and ultimately reform its condition. His early books portray many political and social reformers as well as folk heroes as appropriate instruments. In the last book, he shifts to the poet-prophet, the true artist in any mode, as the necessary means to social equality.

The first book, *Portraits*, responds to the remark by a fellow student, himself German-American: "Say, we've never had a Negro epic."[9] Tolson finds precedent for the genre in the Anglo-American literary heritage. His models are, among others, Longfellow, Whittier, Milton, Tennyson, and Poe.[10] His Tennyson is not the melancholy lyricist, but the poet who envisages "the Parliament of man." Tolson emphasizes the Donne of "no man is an island" rather than the metaphysical poet. Edwin Markham and Langston Hughes, mentors and friends, embody the American populist tradition in white and Black. Literature as well as life fostered his epic intention.

The immediate model for *Portraits* is the *Spoon River Anthology* volume, which attempts to tell "the story of an American country town so as to make it the story of the world."[11] Tolson wants to fashion the story of Harlem into a metaphor for the Afro-American. The technique, an extended synecdoche, "gives . . . Negro America its comedy and tragedy in prismatic epitome" ("Notebooks"). His Harlem becomes metonymically the "mecca," "city of refuse," "Nigger-Heaven," "City of Refuge," and "Capital of the Negro world."[12]

When Tolson presents in *Portraits* approximately two hundred characters significant of the Black community, his worldview becomes clear. The tragicomic tone emanates from the assumption that "the basis of racial prejudice in the United States is economic" (*Caviar and Cabbage*, p. 83). He sees the Harlem community, with its great variety of types, classes, and colors, not as the exotic area of "jungle-bunny" fame but as the subject of an "earthy, unromantic and sociological literature."[13] Throughout the book, indirectly and sometimes directly, Tolson advocates the union of the masses, poor white and poor Black, as the solution to racial and class discrimination. The final goal of proletarian unity is an apocalyptic democracy—classless, multiracial, multicultural—an attainable utopia.

The hero of *Portraits* is the "underdog," who might some day understand and assume his own destiny. Those Harlemites who already have such knowledge are more directly heroic. The group includes Big Jim Casey and Zip Lightner, proletarian heroes who live for the union of Black and white workers. But the particularly flawed hero is Vergil Ragsdale who, as his name suggests, is the poet of the people. He shares their exploited condition. Though there are more effective artists, he appears at greatest length. His perspective may most approximate Tolson's view then:

> "Harlem, O Harlem,
> City of the Big Niggers,
> Graveyard of the Dark Masses,
> Soapbox of the Red Apocalypse. . . ."
> *(Portraits, p. 4)*

Sustained by gin and cocaine, Vergil, the dishwasher at Manto's cafe, dreams of completing his epic poem to Harlem.[14] Although he truly foresees his own pathetic death from tuberculosis, he does not predict the real tragedy: an ignorant landlady will burn the poem, his raison d'être, as trash. Still, this character articulates and represents his people's condition as well as imagines their retribution. His life is ambiguous, as is his heroism.

The style of these poems suits Tolson's epic intention. Characters, presented in short vignettes of about a page, represent the great variety of Harlem humanity, from Peg Leg Snelson to Mrs. Alpha Devine to the Black Moses. As with the poems in *Spoon River*, each of these short ones ends with a climax, a dramatic event, a revelation, a statement, or, in many instances, a blues verse. Tolson, influenced by the imagists, relies on presentation more than on commentary. The larger poetic structure of the entire book, however, lacks variety as poem after poem is introduced mechanically. The diction characterizes occasionally the people in dialect and blues, but the larger voice is the narrator's. The latter speaks of the "little man" as victim but assumes an appreciative tone. The poem presents nobly the techniques of survival in a blues style.

Tolson's next book, *Rendezvous with America*, continues the epic intention in a different vein. As the author broadens his thematic concerns from Harlem to various places in America and to the world at large, the social concerns deepen. The subject here is man — Black and white — as revealed through economics, sociology, and psychology. But the heroes are still political and artistic. Such poets as Sandburg and Whitman set precedents for Tolson's celebration of human potential, despite the actual corruption, inequality, and injustice in still flawed America. Democracy, true justice, and multiculture continue to engage him: "These States breed freedom in and in my bone: / I hymn their virtues and their sins atone" (*Rendezvous*, p. 33).

The epic strain here is less obvious than in *Portraits*. Under the impetus of World Ward II,[15] Tolson sees good and evil written large in human affairs. Celebration of American promise and human potential go hand in hand with the praise of such historical figures as Nat Turner, Frederick Douglass, and Harriet Tubman. The book is replete with heroic figures (and some villains) who become symbolic in the literary context — Daniel Boone, Joe Dimaggio, Thomas Paine, Abraham Lincoln, and many more.

How then do these hymns to America and humanity differ from

the art in Rockefeller Center during the 1930s or from Fourth of July oratory? Although the poetry emphasizes American ideals, it escapes from being merely patriotic encomia. The poetry is skill-fully grounded in realistic observation. In many poems from "Ex-Judge at the Bar" to "Vesuvius," Tolson illustrates the "idols of the tribe"[16]—those deliberately fostered myths of race, caste, and class that separate mankind. His optimism takes root in the faith that the masses will eventually see through the snares, shams, and hypocri-sies to a republican ideal. His ironic—sometimes satiric—tone works against any blind faith in the American dream; he reveals frequently through incident, character, or animal imagery the gulf between the dream and reality.

By now he has worked out for himself a poetic ideal. He refers to the "'3 S's of Parnassus'—Sight, Sound, and Sense."[17] Sight con-cerns the look of a poem on a page. He experiments frequently with centered placement, especially of short lines, to emphasize his point. At other times he works a short line against a longer one for visual effect. His second "S" refers to sound. Sensitive to the ear, he writes poetry to be read aloud—he seldom uses an eye-rhyme. His frequent use of parallelism encompasses both sound and sight. The last "S" means "sense," meaning and imagination—chiefly the use of figura-tive language. Tolson's tropes depend on often startling associations or similarities, frequently using personifications and synechdoche to link seemingly opposed realities in a kind of imaginative dialectic.

Some examples of Tolson's figurative language appear in the long title poem, "Rendezvous with America": "his bat cuts a vacuum," "surfed in white acclaim," "scaling the Alpine ranges of drama with the staff of song," "blue-printing the cabala of the airways," "im-prisoning the magic of symphonies with a baton," "enwombing the multiple soul of the New World" (pp. 6–7). Although some of these metaphors are not entirely satisfactory, they do illustrate the quality and kind of Tolson's imagery.

To see the effect of this aesthetic ideal—the sight, sound, mean-ing, and language of a poem beautifully meshed—I shall consider another of *Rendezvous'* long poems, "Dark Symphony," in detail. On the surface, Tolson's theme merely transforms the cliché of the melting pot into the onomatopoeia of symphonic movement. Called on ode by Joy Flasch (p. 63), the poem has six sections, each with a different musical direction. The first part, three quatrains long, *Allegro Moderato*, moves visually down the page like a series of "s's."

The long line, the short line to the left, and the long line, short line to the right, play against each other. While the metric scheme has the long lines in each stanza and the short lines rhyming, the initial line of each stanza does not do so. There is some alliteration.

In such a poem the names Crispus Attucks and Patrick Henry are expected but not so the lines, "the vertical / Transmitting cry," and "No Banquo's ghost can rise / Against us now" (p. 37). Such obvious metaphors as "the juggernauts of despotism" and "hobnailed Man" and "thorns of greed / On Labor's brow" (p. 37) are offset by "dust is purged to create brotherhood" (p. 37). The stanzas are controlled through their parallel structure and by the musical movement.

The next section, *"Lento Grave,"* details the pathos of those who perform spirituals emblematic of their condition:

> Black slaves singing *One More River to Cross*
> In the torture tombs of slave-ships,
> Black slaves singing *Steal Away to Jesus*
> In jungle swamps.   (p. 38)

Here again Tolson controls rhythm through the musical direction and the parallel structure, as one line of each couplet, the "Black slaves," ends with the title of a spiritual; the following line indicates the symbolic place where it is sung.

The third section, *"Andante Sostenuto,"* counterpoints the previous stanza's slave songs to Psalm 136 (137 in Protestant bibles), which calls to mind the Jewish Babylonian captivity. Each of the three stanzas opens and closes with a repetend, the first two with "They tell us to forget," and the third with "Oh, how can we forget?" Here the expected indictment of racial discrimination in America occurs, but the effective Biblical echo and analogue transcend mere cliché; "They who have shackled us / Require of us a song" recalls Psalm 136. The climactic, "Oh, how can we forget" recalls the Psalmist's "How could we sing a song of the Lord in a foreign land?"

The fourth part, with the direction *"Tempo Primo,"* turns to the New Negro, "Hard-muscled, Fascist-hating, Democracy ensouled," who becomes an ideal of Democracy through his identification with Afro-American heroes. This generic Black signifies his race's contribution by referring to the work done by the slave and free Black masses throughout American history. Their contributions appear in the parallel structure which controls the Whitmanesque categories of Black labor. The section ends with the inevitable stanza showing the New Negro's striding toward the Promised Land of Tomorrow (p. 40). [18]

"*Larghetto*," the fifth section, returns to the first section's satire on white lip service to Democracy. The repetend in each of the four sestets exempts Blacks from particular hypocrisies: "None in the Land can say / To us black men Today" (p. 40).

The final section's *March Tempo* works well through the stanzas of iambic tetrameter and the oft-repeated short line, "We advance!" (p. 43) recalling "The Underdog" (*Portraits*) in the call to unite. In "Dark Symphony," with the irregular rhyme schemes, varied meters, repetitions, and word placements on the page, Tolson illuminates the stock subjects, at least for Black poets during the twenties and thirties. For him, such topics shape themselves into the art epic.

Throughout *Rendezvous*, with few exceptions (there are very few private poems), Tolson practices oratorical rhetoric and evinces social concern. Here the reader encounters a variety of styles in the four long poems, "Rendezvous with America," "Dark Symphony," "Of Men and Cities," and "Tapestries of Time." There is still greater experimentation in the short poems grouped in sections including free verse, Shakespearean sonnet, ballad, and ballade. One poem in iambic monometer, "Song for Myself," is a poetic tour de force, as the diversity in poetic forms increases.

Even where there may be a dramatic incident, or a striking character in the short poems, it has a parabolic effect in building to a climax. The effective "Ballad of the Rattlesnake" is framed by another poem which portrays Black and white sharecroppers. Although they extend now beyond the specific Harlem community, Tolson's concerns remain now in the deeper structure, the same as those in *Portraits* earlier, but they take shape in both conventional and unconventional metrics. In the long and more complex poems, he uses devices that are both poetic and oratorical, including repetition with variation, striking metaphors, and wide-ranging allusions. He subsumes the Black sermon into the artistic voice, and it readdresses the cultural concern. The rhetorical triangle which binds the folk source, the independent imagination, and the appreciative audience continues unbroken.

Besides the American promise and the proletarian expectation, there is another heroic element. Here appears the figure of the bard. "The Poet" portrays a generalized figure who, though largely disregarded in his time, looks uncaringly into the nature of things:

> An Ishmaelite
> He breaks the icons of the Old and New
> . . . . . .
> The poet's lien exempts the Many nor the Few

and

> A champion of the People versus Kings —
> His only martyrdom is poetry:
> A hater of the hierarchy of things —
> Freedom's need is his necessity.
>   (*Rendezvous*, p. 29)

The proud "Ishmaelite" and "anchoret" intuits a "bright new world." Heroic in insight, he dedicates himself to the communication of his vision, which penetrates custom. He reincarnates the Vergil Ragsdale figure, but without the same locale and pathetic circumstances. In *Rendezvous* the Ethiopian Bard of Addis Ababa is equally a kind of prophet. From insight into contemporaneity, he foresees the "bright new world." Lyric vision and social celebration merge.

> His name is an emblem of justice
> Greater than *lumot* of priest
> . . . . . .
> The seven league boots of his images
> Stir the palace and marketplace.
>   (*Rendezvous*, p. 84)

These two, poet and prophet, fuse in Tolson's great man or genius. Tolson saw heroes and villains as representative of human potential for greatness and evil. To serve this social vision, his style evolved with many of the characteristics of oratorical rhetoric.

During his time spent at Columbia University (1931–32) and Greenwich Village (1930s), Tolson became acquainted with the first wave of the moderns represented by Sandburg, Hughes, and Masters. On his own he discovered Eliot's *The Waste Land* and later Crane's *The Bridge* which, according to Mrs. Tolson, "showed her husband that he was 'on the wrong road.'"[19] He therefore set out, still on his own, to come to terms with this academic style:

> Imitation must be in technique only. We have a rich heritage of folklore and history. We are a part of America. We are a part of the world. Our native symbols must be lifted into the universal. Yes, we must study the techniques of Robert Lowell, Dylan Thomas,

Carlos Williams, Ezra Pound, Karl Shapiro, W.H. Auden. The greatest revolution has not been in science but in poetry. We must study such magazines as *Partisan Review*, the *Sewanee Review*, *Accent*, the *Virginia Quarterly*. We must read such critics as Crowe Ransom, Allen Tate, Stephen Spender, George Dillon and Kenneth Burke. (Flasch, *Tolson*, p. 70)[20]

In the period between the publication of *Rendezvous* and the writing of *Libretto*, Tolson included in his eclectic reading the moderns who set the tone of the two decades between the world wars. The reading and the public occasion of Liberia's centenary resulted in the style and content of *Libretto*. In the poem packed with Eliotic notes, we have Tolson's venture in a style aimed at the literary caviar.[21]

Here his view extends from Liberia and Africa to the world. The hero is, symbolically, Liberia, one of only two uncolonized nations in Africa then. Tolson reflects on this historical fact,[22] on Liberia's contribution to Allied efforts in World War II, and on the history of this republic founded by American Blacks freed from slavery; he therefore celebrates its national identity. The epic qualities from *Portraits* and *Rendezvous* reappear here in a different context. Liberia, historically exploited by France and England, aids these two countries by supplying rubber and providing airports during the war. The campaign against "fascists" becomes almost a holy war. Liberia, the name and motto signifying freedom, emerges as both real and symbolic. Transcending racial and economic biases, it foreshadows Africa's triumph in the world. Tolson thus fuses epic material and "academic" style.[23]

The poem is either an ode or a series of eight odes.[24] The titles of metrically varying sections range the diatonic scale from "Do" to "Do." The sections are thematically and symbolically interconnected in the ode form:

Metrically, the term ode usually implies considerable freedom in the introduction of varied rhythmic movements and irregularities of verse-length and rhyme-distribution. There is something "oratorical" about a true ode; and its irregularities may be conceived of as produced by its adaptation to choric rendition or to public declamation, either actual or imagined. . . . Primarily, it [ode] refers to the content and spirit of a poem, implying a certain largeness of thought, continuity of theme, and exalted feeling.[25]

Tolson, faced with the problem of writing an occasional poem about a little-known nation, turns deliberately to the ancient form.

Besides the real and symbolic Liberia, there is a lesser heroic image in the poet-visionary. Because for Tolson man complexly fuses the biological, the sociological, and the psychological, only the Ishmaelite poet knows him deeply. Knowing humanity, historical and contemporary, the poet-prophet discerns the future. Tolson embodies human history in the ferris wheel symbol, which subsumes empires and nations. They rise and fall, alternating decadence and "bright new beginnings." To escape the cyclic nature of power, Tolson asserts through the protagonist[26] that humankind must advance teleologically to a classless utopia. Liberia therefore marks the vanguard, the poet-prophet being instrumental to the movement.

The style reveals a formal polish and philosophical weight in a broad reference which requires pages of notes.[27] Some elements descend directly from earlier techniques, such as Tolson's love of word play, his use of neologism, and his extensive allusions.[28] Once more he uses parallel structure to control the verse. Such elements, all subject to the "3 S's," mark the Tolsonian style.

The first and final "Do" illuminate the manner. The first sets out the principal themes in the attempt to define the meaning of Liberia. A centered question, "Liberia?" highlights the dominant image. In each eight-line stanza, there follows a negation of some cliché: "micro-footnote," "barker's bio-accident," "pimple on the chin of Africa," "caricature with a mimic flag," and "wasteland" (Europe) or "de-stooled elite" (Africa). After a denial, the fifth line in each stanza recenters the definition around the repetend "You are." In regular rhyme-schemes the metrically irregular verses relate Liberia to Europe as lightning rod and Canaan's key and "The rope across the abyss. . . ." Images abound as definition proceeds; Liberia is a metonym spatially to "The Orient of Colors everywhere," philosophically to "*Liberatas* flayed and naked by the road," mythically to "Black Lazarus risen from the White Man's grave," and nationally to "American genius uncrowned in Europe's charnel-house." The final two lines indicate how the nation eludes logical definition: "Liberia and not Liberia, / A moment of the conscience of mankind!" (pp. 13–15).[29]

The poem, unlike earlier ones, minimizes direct, hortatory rhetoric. Allusions help structure and codify meanings. Here the tagends of quotation as well as infusions from different languages including Spanish, French, German, Italian, Latin, Russian, Greek, Turkish, and Hebrew, complicate a line already abstruse. So do the African languages. Symbols like the *Hohere*, the ferris wheel, the merry-go-round, and the tiny republic enrich the verse.

The first section reveals the tone and many of the poetic devices which recur throughout the verse. Liberia has survived the exploitation of Western colonizers. Although its freedom is "flayed and naked," the ideal lives on in promise. "Liberia and not Liberia," the dialectic, the tension of opposites plays throughout the ode. It leads from the initial poem of definition through those which describe the nation's founding ("Mi," "Sol," "La,") to the relationship to France, Britain, and the United States ("Fa," "Ti"). Finally, it widens to classic African civilization ("Re") and the masses everywhere ("Ti" and *passim*). Tolson resolves the tension in "Africa-To-Be" (second "Do" and *passim*).

In the long last section ("Do"), Tolson crafts languages and symbols into a vision of Africa's bright future. Through the metaphors of the automobile, train, and ship, as well as the airplane, he aesthetically transports Liberia, Africa, and the world to an apocalyptic Pluralism. Africa saves itself (p. 53) as well as Europe, America, and Australia. Africa achieves the cosmopolis, *Hohere*, through the United African Nations' cooperation in "polygenetic metropolises polychromatic." The Parliament of African Peoples[30] redeems both the elite and the masses.

The final "Do" sums up the significance of the Liberian experience. It evokes the future in verse that changes from sestet through staggered unrhymed couplets, to centered patterns (p. 47, ll. 555–57) and finally to prose poetry (pp. 48–55, ll. 575–770). The final "Do" thickens with fragments in different languages, references to African as well as European and American thought. Why does the ode, despite the chillingly simple poem, "Fa" (ominous in its simplicity), end in prose paragraphs? Possibly, oratory and Tolson's notion of climax[31] coincide here.

The entire ode moves to a climax as each of the eight sections achieves a minor affirmation. While the first "Do" climaxes in the symbolic definition ("A moment of the conscience of mankind"), the final "Do" declares a new beginning ("the Rosh Hashana of the Africa calends"). And it silences doubters: "*Honi soit qui mal y pense!*" Yet Tolson does not deny the corruption in society and the individual. While "profit" and "avarice" continue, the masses are on a merry-go-round of the "unparadised" who have nowhere to go. The gorged snake, the bird of prey, and the tiger wait in a false peace to strike again. And African nations still wear "Nessus shirts from Europe on their backs" (p. 38).

Tolson's last book of poetry, *Harlem Gallery*, fuses the early subject matter of *Portraits* with his later techniques. Although he presents mechanically more than two hundred Harlemites in *Portraits*, he abandons the strategy here in favor of a much more dynamic one. A number of poems are thematically integrated into the one irregular ode. A different letter of the Greek alphabet labels each of the twenty-four poems in order, just as the names of notes mark *Libretto*. Both poems work toward a signed and structured climax.

The ode incorporates Tolson's epic principle. He has viewed *Harlem Gallery: Book I, the Curator* as the first of five works that would delineate Afro-American history from the African origins to the contemporary world. He has intended to "analogize the history of the Hebrew people in the episodes of the Old Testament as regards persons, places, and events. The dominant idea of the *Harlem Gallery* will be manifest" ("Notebooks"). According to the plan, Book II, Egypt Land, is to be an analogue for the Slave Trade and Southern Bondage; Book III, the Red Sea, an analogue for the Civil War; Book IV, The Wilderness, an analogue for Reconstruction, and Book V, The Promised Land, an analogue for the race's present existence: "a gallery of highbrows and middlebrows and lowbrows against the ethnological panorama of contemporary America" ("Notebooks").

In *Portraits* the once-mentioned Curator places the book's characters on his gallery walls. His voice is unheard throughout the book. The protagonist in *Libretto* (p. 76 n. to l. 554) speaks in the two "Do's" and possibly throughout the entire ode, but the primary text does not develop him.[32] In *Harlem Gallery* the Curator is continually present. Here, too, he has his gallery, though his paintings do not represent the characters in the ode.

While the protagonist in *Libretto* is undramatized throughout the ode, the Curator is a real persona, appearing in significant places like the Zulu Club, meditating on art and life, and interacting with various others. His gallery, though symbolic, is real with regents, gallery-goers, pictures on the four walls, and real curators. The last ones include himself and his alter-ego, Dr. Obi Nkomo. Tolson combines the Curator in *Portraits*, a speaker who is scarcely even a framing device, and the protagonist in *Libretto*, possibly the consciousness through which the poem is played. This evolution marks the current curator.

The Harlem Gallery is a firmer and more centralized metaphor than was Liberia. Harlem appears less now through representation than through evocation. As with Liberia and America in the earlier books, the area is both place and symbol. It maintains historicity but assumes a larger meaning. Although the numbers of characters are fewer, major figures are more deeply probed. Harlem the social place becomes Harlem the human type.

The figures of Vergil Ragsdale (*Portraits*), the poet, Good Grey Bard (*Rendezvous*), and the Bard of Timbuktu (*Libretto*) become fused and enlarged here. The artists evoke both their personal and public lives. The division between private failure and public assurance in the aesthetic vocation, evident even in Ragsdale, appears uniquely human. Harlem, a nexus of Afro-American artist-heroes, shares the inhabitants' ambivalent and tragicomic blues. The inhabitants suit well the modern epic:

> in this race, at this time, in this place,
> to be a Negro artist is to be
> a flower of the gods, whose growth
> is dwarfed at an early stage —
> a Brazilian owl moth,
> a giant among his own in an acreage
> dark with the darkman's designs,
> where the milieu moves back downward like the sloth.
> (*Harlem Gallery*, p. 153)

Tolson even maintains the abstract hero and symbolizes Art itself, but the hero no longer strides with the masses toward an apocalyptic new earth. Tolson has his concept of an economically determined world transmuted by true art. The true artist foreshadows the new world not as the "Futurafrique" (*Libretto*), but as the "dusk of dawn." The artistic subsumes the political. Art, like John Laugart's "Black Bourgeoisie," so long as authentic, becomes sanative.

The style of the ode is more dynamic than that in *Libretto*. The new mode, with allusiveness and complexity of metaphor, image and symbol, excludes verbiage. Here emerge greater mastery and flexibility.[33] The poems project their themes through a flux of character, interaction, and talk. The peripatetic Curator goes to Laugart's apartment, Aunt Grindle's Chitterling Shop, the Harlem Gallery, and the Zulu Club. He hears or knows about the happenings at the police station, the Haha Club, and the Angelus Funeral Home. His wanderings focus the geography of Harlem. His thoughts about the characters, life, and art are projected in both discursive and narrative cantos. At once a dramatic persona and an undramatized prophet like Eliot's Tiresias, he represents the consciousness through which the ode is played. In a sense he "makes" the "autobio-fragment" — the ode itself — literally humanize intellect and oratory. The poem ends then with the achievement of the metonym:

> The allegro of the Harlem Gallery
> is not a chippy fire,
> for here, in focus, are paintings that chronicle
> a people's New World odyssey
> from chattel to Esquire!
> *(Harlem Gallery*, p. 173)

Some indication of how Tolson's poem works can be seen in the first canto. In "Alpha," one hears the voice of the Curator for the first time. The basic symbols appear in the first two lines (p. 19):

> The Harlem Gallery, an Afric pepper bird,
> awakes me at a people's dusk of dawn.

The Harlem Gallery, like the pepper bird native to Africa, stirs the Curator to action. He must envision the ode, the "autobio-fragment," at a people's dusk of dawn,[34] the transition between night and morning symbolically figuring a new socio-economic age. Here the Afro-American will attain his full stature. The ode itself will both prophetically and aesthetically help to usher this in.

Then the poem evokes some Third World challenges to the "Great White World," the former being the social equivalent to the Curator's craft. Introspectively, the Curator turns to himself, faces the task, and sees himself as flawed, being comic where seriousness is called for, being serious when comedy is required. He shares humankind's meandering approach to the necessary search for true freedom. He envisions the task again, now hearing "a dry husk-of-locust" blues asking "Black Boy, O Black Boy, / is the port worth the cruise?" Inhibitions based on self-doubt harden the task; to maintain the integrity of self, humanity, and race proves nearly too much. The "clockbird's jackass laughter" haunts his effort. Challenged by the pepper bird, but mocked by the clockbird, he reveals the spirit of transitional man in a transitional world.

As in "Alpha" the entire ode centers in irregular rhyme, internal rhyme, alliteration, assonance, and consonance. Major symbols in the ode, such as Harlem Gallery, African pepper bird, Dusk of Dawn, and clockbird, recur now. The Buridan's ass and "the gaffing *To ti*" have appeared earlier in different genres, but images of the Hambletonian gathering for a leap, the apples of Cain, and barrel cactus are fresh. Here closes the decade long evolution in his worldview as an Afro-American, for his craft subsumes and perfects his oratory.

But with an epic intention, why does he abandon the folk model for the academic one? Why, if so committed to the Black and white masses, does he write in the style of the literary elite?

Perhaps *Harlem Gallery* is not exclusively for the elite. Here one reads and enjoys with persistence more than with erudition. Or, maybe Tolson regards the style as a criterion of excellence. Perhaps he wants to master the technique but to maintain his Afro-American experience. A final answer comes from Tolson, himself one of the "crafty masters of social conscience"[35]:

> Today
> The Few
> Yield Poets
> Their due;
> Tomorrow
> The Mass
> Judgment
> Shall Pass.
> (*Rendezvous*, p. 50)

NOTES

1. *Caviar and Cabbage: Selected Columns by Melvin B. Tolson from the Washington Tribune, 1937–1944* by Robert M. Farnsworth (Columbia: Univ. of Missouri Press, 1982), 29. Hereafter cited in the notes as *C. and C.* Quotations by permission of the Univ. of Missouri Press; Copyright 1980 by the Curators of the Univ. of Missouri.

2. Ibid., 53: "At his best, the old preacher had the poetry of words and motion. . . ."

3. Farnsworth sees a melding of Christianity and Radicalism in Tolson; see ibid., Introduction, 5–6 and Sec. I.

4. Melvin B. Tolson, *A Gallery of Harlem Portraits*, ed. Robert M. Farnsworth (Columbia: Univ. of Missouri Press, 1979). Hereafter cited as *Portraits*. Quotations by permission of the Univ. of Missouri Press; copyright 1979 by the Curators of the Univ. of Missouri.

5. Melvin B. Tolson, *Rendezvous with America* (New York: Dodd, Mead, 1944). Hereafter cited as *Rendezvous*.

6. Melvin B. Tolson, *Libretto for the Republic of Liberia* (London: Collier-Macmillan, 1970). Hereafter cited as *Libretto*.

7. Melvin B. Tolson, *Harlem Gallery: Book I, the Curator* (New York: Twayne, 1965). Hereafter cited in the notes as *H.G.*

8. Tolson pursued many of these ideas in his newspaper columns and in unpublished novels and plays. One can find essentially the same ideas in different genres.

9. A concept that Tolson pursued in "The Ape of God" in which he explicates the characteristics and functions of the artist-visionary. Material will be found in Tolson's unpublished Notebooks and Papers in the Manuscript Room, Library of Congress. Hereafter cited as "Notebooks."

10. Frost, Whitman, Hughes, Wright, and Sterling Brown are also part of the American literary tradition celebrating the "common man." Tolson had a familiarity with these authors.

11. Babette Deutsch, *Poetry in Our Time: A Critical Survey of Poetry in the English-Speaking World 1900 to 1960* 2d ed. (New York: Doubleday, 1963), 48.

12. Tolson uses all these names in one version of the opening poem in *Portraits*; "Harlem," *The Arts Quarterly*, I (April–June 1937), 27.

13. Melvin B. Tolson, "The Harlem Group of Negro Writers," master's thesis, Columbia Univ., 1940, p. 121.

14. Thus constituting an epic within an epic as Tolson was later to do in "Upsilon," *H.G.*, in which the smaller poem complements the larger one.

15. Tolson was originally much opposed to American entry into World War II but later changed his opinion. See *C. and C.* and *passim*.

16. "Idols of the Tribe," a term derived from Francis Bacon's *Novum Organum*, is a metaphor that becomes symbolic in Tolson's treatment.

17. The three S's of Parnassus were first developed as an ideal for his poetry in the 1930s. See Joy Flasch, *Melvin B. Tolson* (New York: Twayne, 1972), 48 and *passim*. Hereafter cited as Flasch, *Tolson*.

18. Such an ending, looking to the future, is typical of Tolson.

19. Interview with Mrs. Ruth Tolson, Washington, D.C., 23 Oct. 1974.

20. See also Tolson in "A Poet's Odyssey," *Anger and Beyond: The Negro Writer in the United States*, ed. Herbert Hill (New York: Harper and Row, 1966), 195. Besides Eliot, Yeats, Baudelaire, and Pasternak, Tolson studied "all the great moderns."

21. Tolson remarked about his "The Man Inside": "It was not written for

you, like 'Caviar and Cabbage.' It was written about you. It speaks to those super-intellectuals who whoop it up for democracy," *C. and C.*, 229. This illustrates his conscious preparation of form to accommodate different audiences.

22. Tolson in "Notebooks" states: "Start horizontally from fact to metaphor: then the idea moves vertically from metaphor to symbol at the apex of the language."

23. Since the *Libretto* jacket blurb calls the poem an "African Odyssey" and "this epic masterpiece," there is some indication of Tolson's intention.

24. See Flasch, *Tolson*, p. 75: "The *Libretto* is a long ode consisting of eight sections . . . "; see also Jon Woodson, "A Critical Analysis of the Poetry of Melvin B. Tolson," doctoral diss., Brown Univ., 1978: "the poem, consisting of eight Pindaric odes . . ." 110. This same difference of opinion occurs about *H.G.*, called an ode by Flasch. "*Harlem Gallery* is structured so that there is an ode for each letter of the ancient Greek alphabet . . ." Woodson, 195.

25. J.F.A. Pyre, "A Short Introduction to English Versification," Appendix, *English Poetry of the Nineteenth Century*, ed. Oscar Campbell and J.F.A. Pyre (New York: Appleton-Century-Crofts, 1929), 754.

26. Woodson points out the existence of the protagonist: "Note 367 contains, besides note 554, the only direct assertion that the poem, consisting of eight Pindaric odes — thus presumably spoken by someone — contains a protagonist. Tolson's protagonist, in contrast to Eliot's identification of the seer Tiresias as 'a mere spectator and not indeed a "character" . . . ' is not anywhere named. . . . The reader of the *Libretto* is provided no key as to whom the protagonist might be" (pp. 110–11). See entire discussion, pp. 110–13.

27. Tolson's notes, like Eliot's, still leave much of the work of deciphering the poem to the reader.

28. Tolson's reading habits were essentially eclectic: "The worst thing you can do if you expect to get through a college or university is to pattern your reading after mine. I have reading sprees. I may get to thinking about snakes and spend weeks studying rattlers, cobras, pythons, Gilas, and chameleons. . . . Or I may start on a reading spree that covers the history of undertakers," *C. and C.*, 166.

29. Tolson here builds on his earlier poetry in his use of the technique of repetition with a twist and/or reversal in the final repetend.

30. "The poet Tennyson dreamed of a Parliament of Man, a Federation of the World. I cast my vote for that," *C. and C.*, 127. See also Tennyson, "Locksley Hall."

31. See discussion of "climax," Flasch, *Tolson*, p. 76 and Tate, *Libretto*, p. 10.

32. For full discussion of protagonist and his relationship to the content of poem, see Woodson, ch. 3.

33. All the poems in *H.G.* are centered.

34. "Dusk of Dawn" is the title of W.E.B. Du Bois' autobiography. For a longer discussion see Mariann Russell, *Melvin B. Tolson's* Harlem Gallery: *A Literary Analysis* (Columbia: Univ. of Missouri Press, 1980), 54, 67.

35. Jane Kramer, "In the Garrison," *New York Review of Books* (2 Dec. 1982), 8.

Jon Woodson

Melvin Tolson and the Art of Being Difficult

A poem must be an enigma for the vulgar, chamber-music for the initiated.

Stéphane Mallarmé, *Magie*

I.

They can pile up records and labels a mile high, and in the end they will find, pinned under that pile, not me but their own intelligence.

Jean Toomer, *The Wayward and the Seeking:*
A Collection of Writings by Jean Toomer

In his essay *On Difficulty* George Steiner says, "Far more often than not we signify by 'a difficulty' something that 'we need to look up.'"[1] Similarly, the approach to the difficulties of Melvin Tolson's "dense allusive" poetry has consistently sent his critics to reference sources. It is an assumption easily come by that the solution to difficulties in poems like *Harlem Gallery* is simply a matter of taking the time to look up the unfamiliar words, the names of pagan deities, and the locations of exotic cities. Having removed these obstacles, readers should be able to find out what the poet is trying to say; Steiner confirms this: "Our resort to the authority of the dictionary is precisely analogous to that which we perform when translating from a foreign tongue."[2] In this way of looking at Tolson's poetry, the difficulties may eventually be eradicated by "homework." But in the process one must first clarify the intellectual legacy of the Harlem Renaissance as well as the significant sources, including the mystic

Gurdjieff and the novelist Jean Toomer. The method combines literary history with textual inquiry.

The resort to looking everything up as a means for clearing up Tolson's difficulties is explicit in a statement by Dudley Randall, who says that "If the reader has a well-stored mind or is willing to use dictionaries, encyclopedias, atlases, and other reference books," Tolson's poetry "should present no great difficulty."[3] Having presumably made his translation, Randall finds that reading Tolson's poetry is like reading other "learned poets such as Milton and T.S. Eliot." In his very thorough critical history of Afro-American poetry, *Drumvoices*, Eugene Redmond quotes what Randall has said; however, Redmond notes that the rewards are markedly different:

> . . . reading Tolson is not *exactly* like reading other learned poets, for he places black information in front of the reader. He bends the ode into an Afro-American musical structure and celebrates the black past.[4]

Redmond has presumably been able to read the poetry and has found in it an ideological and cultural message that he can assign to a period in the sociological development of Afro-American literary thought:

> Hence Tolson extends, sometimes in camouflage, his ideas about man's similarities and differences. To be sure, he *is* saying that black men and white men *are* different — but that the differences are not significant enough to keep them from working together for the mutual good. This particular stand, which laces the work of Hayden, Tolson, Hughes, and early Gwendolyn Brooks, is not one that will remain popular among poets who subscribe to the black aesthetic of the 1960s.[5]

The statement is certainly curious and is not at all convincing. What does "sometimes in camouflage" mean? Redmond has worked out Tolson's meaning by associating the poet with the ideas that belong to his time. Redmond sounds defensive ("to be sure"), as though he has not been able to locate a meaning for Tolson's poetry and so has assigned one. The treatment is rather the rule than the exception.

Wilburn Williams, Jr., believes that it is possible to read Tolson. The poet, it turns out, is talking about life and "his heroes are always men of common sense."[6] Williams believes that critics who share S.W. Fabio's negative view of Tolson have overlooked Tolson's accomplishments: Tolson is "true to the wit, humor, and raciness of black speech."[7] At the same time, Tolson is a master of the modernist style. Williams ends his essay by informing us that reading Tolson is a matter of spending the time to look things up:

> But, one protests, the poem *is* difficult to read. . . . A poem like *Harlem Gallery* is not to be read all at once. Tolson would agree with Barthes that a single reading of a work is no reading at all; even though Tolson sees the single reading as the text's assault on the reader rather than the reader's defilement of the text. . . .[8]

The difficulty of a text is not as simple as it might seem. George Steiner sets forth four classes in his essay:

> Contingent difficulties aim to be looked up; modal difficulties challenge the inevitable parochialism of honest empathy; tactical difficulties endeavor to deepen our apprehension by dislocating and goading to new life the supine energies of word and grammar. Each of these three classes of difficulty is a part of the contract of ultimate or preponderant intelligibility between poet and reader, between text and meaning. . . . *Ontological* difficulties confront us with blank questions about the nature of human speech, about the status of significance, about the necessity and purpose of the construct which we have, with more or less rough and ready consensus, come to perceive as a poem.[9]

Each of these four categories of difficulties may be said to be applicable to Tolson's poetry, and the importance of any category may vary depending upon the skills, sensibilities, and backgrounds that readers bring to bear on the poems. To say that *Harlem Gallery* may be deciphered by means of looking things up is to indicate a procedure that overlaps two categories of difficulties — contingent and ontological — and ignores the possibility that the poem lacks a fixed framework of ideas or images.

The questions about the meaning of Tolson's poems remain. So does the question, "How can Tolson's poetry be analyzed by looking things up until some organizing principle has been discovered?" Without the organizing principle or the pattern of reference, the analysis consists of the reader's assumptions masquerading as the poet's ideas. In Tolson's poetry, in *Libretto for the Republic of Liberia* and *Harlem Gallery* especially, nothing is inherently "obvious"; values, beliefs, and views cannot be assigned to the poet because of their likelihood or by association. It is perhaps possible to find a key by means of deduction, but so far this has not worked in the case of Tolson's complex, allusive, and esoteric poetry.

II.

But rather than a betrayal of race for a cheap chauvinism, Toomer's poetic resolution of his private and public quest for identity represents a genuine effort to cast off all classifications that enslave human beings and inhibit the free play of intelligence and goodwill in the world.

Bernard W. Bell

During the brief period that Melvin Tolson lived in Harlem — the 1931–32 academic year — he attended Columbia University and wrote a master's thesis on the Harlem writers. The work, *The Harlem Group of Negro Writers*, encompassed only those individuals Tolson personally knew, though this is a somewhat curious restriction as the thesis is composed of plot outlines and paraphrases of reviews and does not reflect Tolson's personal acquaintance with the Harlem writers. Joy Flasch has noted the influence of the acquaintances:

> Tolson referred to these writers [Countee Cullen, Langston Hughes, Claude McKay, Walter White, Eric Walrond, Rudolph Fisher, Jessie Fauset, George Schuyler, W.E.B. DuBois, James Weldon Johnson, and Wallace Thurman] . . . in his lectures around the country, and in his poetry.[10]

The tendency has been to see Melvin Tolson as an idiosyncratic poet, but clearly the view has not contributed toward the understanding of his poetry; though Tolson's associations have been acknowledged, they have not been used to try to understand what Tolson was doing. The difficulty has come about because of a general confusion on the part of critics about the meaning of the entire cultural movement known as the Harlem Renaissance. Because it is so difficult to evaluate the period, it is hard to see clearly the relationship of any writer to that movement; in this vein, Wilburn Williams states:

> Although he was a member of that generation of black poets who burst upon the scene in the Harlem Renaissance of the 1920s, and although he was the friend of many of those poets, Tolson never

became identified with any particular literary movement. When one recalls the name of Langston Hughes, a host of other black writers immediately come to mind — Countee Cullen, Arna Bontemps, Wallace Thurman, and many more. This is not the case with Tolson. Tolson was both a late-comer and a loner.[11]

The Harlem writers were linked by time, place, and friendships, not by any uniformity of aesthetic principles. Tolson may have been a late-comer, but he in some definite ways saw himself as linked to the Harlem Group: he wrote two books of poetry about Harlem and Harlem artists, he wrote a master's thesis about the Harlem Group, and he continued to speak about the Harlem writers throughout his life. His association was a profound experience which shaped the poetry that he would write many years later.

Perhaps the best indication of what he was introduced to in Harlem appears in Wallace Thurman's satire of the Harlem Group, *Infants of the Spring*. When Thurman came to write this novel, the excitement about Harlem's Black culture had cooled. There was a Depression, and life looked much different than it did in 1925, the year *The New Negro* was published.

Thurman's *Infants of the Spring* shows that the Harlem artists were very much held together by friendships; the bonds allowed men and women, who actually agreed on very little as concerned art or politics, to overlook their differences in the name of a common commitment to their racial mission as artists. Their social unity was a product of their wish to be New Negroes. Thurman's novel shows this "Niggerati," as he calls them, coexisting in a rooming house — Niggerati Manor — and engaging in a constant round of partying and casual sexual affairs.

Raymond, the protagonist of *Infants of the Spring*, is Thurman's mouthpiece; as members of the Harlem Group were able to identify themselves as particular characters in the novel, it is probable that Raymond is Wallace Thurman's self-portrait. Raymond is not pleased with the way the Harlem Renaissance is turning out: ". . . he was disgusted with the way everyone sought to romanticize Harlem and Harlem Negroes."[12] More to the point, Raymond views his associates as not living up to their potentials; they are lazy and produce very little in the way of art. Raymond, who has advertised himself to his friends as a Nietzschean, says at one point that "I know of only one Negro who has the elements of greatness, and that's Jean Toomer."[13] *In-*

fants of the Spring was published in 1932, the year that Melvin Tolson lived in Harlem. Thurman's novel shows that when Tolson met up with the Harlem Group, and particularly in the case of Wallace Thurman, he was confronted with a group of people who had come under the influence of Jean Toomer, the disseminator of a peculiar set of ideas. It is noteworthy that Jean Toomer is not portrayed in *Infants of the Spring* (just as he does not figure in Tolson's thesis on the Harlem Group), but the "Nietzschean" ideas that Raymond espouses in the novel are clearly the ideas that Toomer passed on to Thurman and the others in the Harlem Group who were not too disinterested. The following list represents the complex of ideas which Raymond believes are important.

1. "It is mass movements which bring forth individuals." I don't give a good god damn what becomes of any mass.
2. "And if out of a wholesale allegiance to Communism, the Negro could develop just a half dozen men who were really and truly outstanding, the result would be worth the effort."
3. No intelligent person subscribes to the doctrine of Nordic superiority but everyone can realize that now the white man has both the power and the money. His star is almost at the zenith of its ascendancy. There are signs of an impending eclipse but meanwhile he holds the whip.
4. "The pygmies have taken us over now, and I doubt if any of us has the strength to use them for a step-ladder to a higher plane."
5. Negroes are much like any other human beings. They have the same social, physical, and intellectual divisions.[14]

These ideas and a few others form the core of a body of beliefs shared to varying extents by members of the Harlem Group. One idea missing from the previous list requires that it be mentioned here. A new race, it was believed, was taking form on the American continent. The new cosmic or universal group appears in a number of works of Harlem writing. In a short poem, "The Riddle," by G.D. Johnson and published in 1925, and most exhaustively in George Schuyler's 1933 novel *Black No More*, the creation of the universal race of men is speeded up by means of a fictional scientific process. The idea of a cosmic race recurs in Toomer's poem *Blue Meridian* (1936). The author thought that he was a member:

As I grew up, as I began to develop and differentiate spiritually, as I became psychologically individualized, my expression and even my features underwent a corresponding change. Now, at the present time, they are such that — to judge from the responses I get — I have the appearance of a sort of universal man. According to their own subjective experiences, various people have taken me for American, English, Spanish, French, Italian, Russian, Hindu, Japanese, Romanian, Indian, and Dutch.[15]

The five ideas taken from Thurman's *Infants of the Spring* and the idea of a cosmic American race demonstrate that when Melvin Tolson reached the Harlem Group in 1931, he became familiar with a body of unusual information. The intellectual heart of the Harlem Group and its source is no mystery — these ideas came from Jean Toomer. Ultimately, the ideas that Toomer brought to the Harlem writers were passed on to Melvin Tolson, in whose poetry the ideas at last came to the full expression that none of the other Harlem writers had been able adequately to provide.

Robert Bone, Mabel Dillard, Hugh Gloster, Edward Margolies, and Arna Bontemps say that a major influence on the Harlem Renaissance of the 1920s was the personality, philosophy, and artistry of Jean Toomer, the experimental poet and novelist. Although Toomer's influence is generally agreed upon as being important, the exact nature of the contribution is greatly controversial. Toomer did not long continue in the conventional mode of an Afro-American writer. Because of his shifting attitude toward his own racial identity and his failure as a published author, he has been described as a spiritual exile and an artistic failure. Nevertheless, Toomer, "as the only negro writer of the 1920s who participated on equal terms in the creation of the modern idiom,"[16] brought the Harlem Group into their initial familiarity with the principles of high literary modernism. It was as a modernist writer that Toomer joined the Harlem Group in 1925, but it was the specialized modernism of a literary coterie, including Hart Crane, Waldo Frank, and Gorham Munson. "Obsessed" with the theories of P.D. Ouspensky, the group proposed G.I. Gurdjieff's system of self-development for American artists and intellectuals.

Jean Toomer arrived on the scene in Harlem after spending the summer of 1924 at Gurdjieff's Institute for the Harmonious Development of Man at Fontainebleau, France. Toomer began a program for introducing Gurdjieff's ideas to the Harlem writers, and for some members of the Harlem Group the activities associated with these ideas became the very essence of the movement to which they belonged. The short story "Smoke, Lilies, and Jade," Richard Bruce's stream of consciousness account of the inner world of a Harlem writer, published in the only issue of Wallace Thurman's journal *Fire!*, contains this catalogue of activities:

> . . . to argue and read Wilde . . . Freud . . . Boccaccio and Schnitzler . . . to attend Gurdjieff meetings and know things. . . .[17]

The previous quote demonstrates the degree to which, at least for some individuals, the ideas that Toomer brought into Harlem were part of the fabric of the Harlem Renaissance. Darwin T. Turner summarizes the introduction of Gurdjieff's system into Harlem:

> After a summer's study in 1924 at Gurdjieff's institute in Fontainebleau, France, Toomer returned to America in the fall as a disciple. His earliest efforts to instruct such "New Negro" artists as Wallace Thurman, Dorothy Peterson, Aaron Douglas, and Nella Larsen aborted, according to Langston Hughes, because few Blacks had both the leisure time necessary for the inner observation and the money necessary for the lessons.[18]

Although in a very real sense Toomer's attempt to indoctrinate the Harlem Group may be said to have failed if a permanent organization is the measure of success, this failure was not by any means complete with regard to a permanent change in the psychology of certain individuals. Gurdjieff's entire movement was in a sense abortive, for Gurdjieff was unable to erect a permanent and continuing Institute; despite the institutional lapse, Gurdjieff still continues to influence a large number of individuals through his published writings and through those of his disciples who still survive.

In plain words, Gurdjieff's system was a series of exercises that were designed to maximize human potential, to create superhuman personalities. Many artists and intellectuals throughout the world found this an attractive idea. Jean Toomer was introducing dangerously stimulating ideas to a select group of young, volatile, imaginative experimenters who desired a method for truly becoming "New Negroes." When Melvin B. Tolson arrived in Harlem in the fall of 1931 and was introduced to the Harlem Group of Negro writers, as he named them, what sort of a collection of men and women did he meet up with? This is a rather challenging and controversial question that perhaps cannot be answered. But Toomer was most closely associated with Bontemps, McKay, Aaron Douglas, Hughes, Cullen, Fauset, and Hurston, according to Benson and Dillard's account of Toomer's initial contacts with Harlem writers. Later some of these individuals dropped away, leaving Toomer's inner circle to consist of Douglas, Thurman, Jackman, Larsen, and Peterson. When Tolson arrived in Harlem in 1931, he met and later wrote his thesis on a number of Harlem writers, and that group included Wallace Thurman, one member of Jean Toomer's circle.

There are several indications that Wallace Thurman introduced Melvin Tolson to G.I. Gurdjieff's teachings during Tolson's stay in Harlem. The evidence that points in this direction appears in Tolson's poems, notes, and speeches. The poet hardly refers directly to his interest in Gurdjieff's teachings. The policy keeps with the secret nature of the Gurdjieff "work," as it is often called, for Gurdjieffs's system was not taught outside of closed groups of committed students. Tolson's silence in this regard possibly indicates his dedication to the perpetuation of the esoteric system of thought and action. Throughout Tolson's poetry, and in most of the notes that remain from his lectures and classes, appear many of the penetrating ideas that Gurdjieff disseminated through Jean Toomer and Wallace Thurman. Far from playing a minor role, these truly esoteric ideas were pervasive, forming the essence of what may be called Tolson's philosophy; Tolson traveled throughout the South lecturing, and for a time wrote a newspaper column, all the while putting forth ideas that were thought to have originated with him. What was meant by "inner observation," and what was the nature of the lessons that Jean Toomer brought with him from the Institute for the Harmonious Development of Man? What things did Gurdjieff's students know? Darwin Turner summarizes the teachings:

> Gurdjieff professed to have the ability to help people fuse their fragmented selves into a new and perfect whole—a harmony of mind, body, and soul—through a system of mental and physical exercise emphasizing introspection, meditation, concentration, discipline, and self-liberation.[19]

Turner's description sounds altogether uninspiring. The account is written so as to make readers wonder at the attractiveness of the methods. Yet Toomer and many others were powerfully attracted to Gurdjieff the teacher and equally to his teachings. Toomer was later to write that "with certain notable exceptions, every one of my main ideas has a Gurdjieff idea as a parent."[20] This intellectual debt to Gurdjieff is also a feature of Melvin Tolson's thought, as it is for other followers of esoteric teachings, for Gurdjieff expressed ideas that were thought to be objective and were not to be perverted or altered according to the whim of subjective individuality. They were to be mastered in their pure form, and this feature of esoteric thought is pervasive. W.B. Yeats, the modernist poet and occultist, wrote that "Individuality is not as important as our age has imagined."

In New York City during the early 1920s, Jean Toomer associated with a literary group that, devoted to P.D. Ouspensky, took inspiration from his book *Tertium Organum*. The main thrust was that "mankind was undergoing a type of spiritual decay as the result of materialism that had gripped the Western world."[21] Toomer's style was influenced by the ideas:

> Ouspensky had claimed that the most effective medium for the revelation of spiritual realities was through poetry; and this idea found immediate appeal with Toomer. Toomer, along with the others, believed that poetry ought to encompass a new type of language, and Toomer especially believed that the language and ideas of poetry ought to be necessarily obscure and only hint at partial revelation.[22]

Toomer's aesthetic was based on the requirements of the objective ideas of the esoteric system. Poetry was a vehicle that could be at once obscure and reveal. The difficulties here are both modal and ontological — the reader must be ready to perceive that something lies beyond the difficulties; he must be willing to work through the obstacles that have been placed in his way. A new type of language which only hints at partial revelation fails when it veils too well the meaning. Toomer's attempts to write this way, as seen in *Cane*, fail as do Hart Crane's, when compared to successful works of the type. In the poetry of Melvin Tolson the aesthetic fully takes shape. Toomer and Crane fail largely because they both lacked a sense of humor. Both Tolson and Gurdjieff resorted to satire to embody the esoteric system in literature. In later years Gurdjieff was to write down his system; and in the three books that he produced, the writing only hints at a partial revelation. But he did not write poetry. Melvin Tolson's *Libretto* and *Harlem Gallery* are also successful attempts to record the system that Gurdjieff taught, and Tolson found a way to do what Toomer, Hart Crane, and Wallace Thurman could not do: create a new type of language suitable for the revelation of objective spiritual realities.

III.

> "Great minds require of us a reading glass;
> great souls, a hearing aid."
> Melvin Tolson, *Harlem Gallery*

Today, the exact means by which Melvin Tolson was introduced to Gurdjieff's thought are unknown. A study of Tolson's poetry shows that he was very familiar with P.D. Ouspensky's book *A New Model of the Universe* (1931); it is likely that this book was given to him by Wallace Thurman, Toomer's chief disciple. Jean Toomer, by the time Tolson reached Harlem in 1931, and had moved on, first to the Midwest and the Southwest and by 1931 to Carmel, California. It is noteworthy that Tolson wrote his thesis for his Master's degree at Columbia University on those of the Harlem Group that he was able to meet personally, and thus Toomer is omitted from that study. Although Toomer did not seem to have created a strong organization in Harlem, he does seem to have maintained contact with Thurman. This is not certain, but in December 1934 Wallace Thurman, having just flown back to New York from Hollywood, died of tuberculosis in the charity ward at Bellevue Hospital. Because Jean Toomer was still living in Carmel in 1934, this trip would seem to have been a last trip to visit his teacher. With Thurman's death in 1934, Toomer's last link with the Harlem Group was dissolved. In later years Tolson made trips to New York City as well as to other points in the South, the Midwest, and the East, so the possibility that contact with Gurdjieff groups was maintained by Tolson does exist. One of the mysteries surrounding Tolson was that he did not receive his master's until 1940, even though he had completed everything but his bibliography. The ploy may have allowed him to make trips to New York without raising any questions.

As did many of G.I. Gurdjieff's followers who were poets, Melvin Tolson absorbed the major ideas of Gurdjieff's system into his personality and subsequently passed them on embedded in his poetry. Most of the ideas that are central to Gurdjieff's system for developing human potential are important components of Tolson's thought and turn out to be the themes of his poems. Some of Gurdjieff's ideas were given more emphasis by Tolson than were others; certain ideas were more easily expressed openly, while others required careful disguise. In particular favor was the idea, again, that "Negroes are much like any other human beings. They have the same social, physical, and intellectual divisions." This view, often repeated by Tolson, appears in many of his poems and essays.

With Gurdjieff's teachings an idea could take many forms, and laws or principles often had several names or were expressed through several metaphors. In keeping with this practice, Tolson gave the idea a name of his own, "The Law of Synthetic Identity," and, not stopping there, he called it the concept of "tri-dimensionality." In the notes that he provided for the long psychological poem "E.&.O.E.," he says: "In an attempt to establish his *I-ness* as a Negro—a concept in itself a unity of opposites—the man combines the Cartesian definition with a variant of the Law of Synthetic Identity. This is the key to the allusions in the poem."[23] Tolson did not provide notes to his verses to clear up the contingent difficulties, and many of his notes, as is this one, make matters even worse for the reader; it does not explicate the text; it merely gives some directions whereby the text may be explicated. Only slightly less obscure than the poem, it does direct the reader to consider the Law of Synthetic Identity. Tolson, here, gives no indication of where the reader must look up the law. But it was common knowledge within the Gurdjieff groups; the chart below shows that it expresses the goal of the system, the fusion of fragmented selves into a new and perfect whole—a harmony of mind, body and soul:

Source	Agent	Divisions
Tolson "E.&O.E."	Law of Synthetic Identity, Tridimensionality, I-ness	biological, sociological, psychological
Thurman *Infants of the Spring*	Negroes, human beings	physical, social, intellectual
Toomer *The Gurdjieff Experience*	man has three bodies	physical, emotional, mental

Source	Agent	Divisions
Ouspensky *Tertium Organum*	human beings contain in themselves the following three categories	the body, the soul, the region of the unknown consciousness; the one I, potential in the ordinary man
Gurdjieff *The Herald of Coming Good*	the development of man is out of harmony	body, emotions, mind being, knowledge, will

The chart shows that Tolson's "I-ness" is the equivalent of P.D. Ouspensky's "the one I" and that these terms expressed the potential in man for the achievement of wholeness. The chart also shows that Tolson's concept of an "'I-ness' that could not be encompassed by his 'Negro-ness,'"[24] derived from Ouspensky's version of the concept rather than that of Gurdjieff, Toomer, or Thurman, for Ouspensky makes the further elaboration that it is within "the region of the unknown consciousness" — the psychological division in Tolson's version — that the development of the individual must be fulfilled. Furthermore, the chart shows that the concept of man's dividedness becomes more abstract as the concept moved from the transliterated Armenian of Gurdjieff, who did not speak English when he began to teach in Britain and France, to the academic jargon of Melvin Tolson, the college teacher. One suspects that Tolson's intent in propounding his laws and his "tridimensionality" is on one hand somewhat ironic and on the other intentionally obscure. Joy Flasch quotes from the notebook of one of Tolson's students: "Every person is a tridimensionality: biological, sociological, psychological."[25] This "tridimensionality" of Tolson's causes man to lack a real, unified "I" and thus man has a "synthetic identity." In *Harlem Gallery* ("ETA") Tolson shows how life prevents the common man from achieving self-unification.

> Doctor Nkomo sighed: / "The nicks and cuts under a stallion's tail / spur him to carry it higher: / but the incised horsetail of a man / drains the bones of his I-ness drier."

Gurdjieff constantly stressed the importance of achieving this unity of the self into a real "I"; J.G. Bennett states that:

> Gurdjieff in many places insists that man has no I and no will. Indeed, in the same chapter in which this passage occurs, he illustrates in a very telling way the absence of the 'supposed will' in

man. This often creates misunderstandings. It is necessary to understand that the fourth part of man, his 'I', is indeed his 'will' but, owing to the faulty conditions of education, man reaches adulthood without his own 'will', which is the same as saying without his own 'I'. The place of 'will' and the way by which the 'will' in man can be developed, is seldom discussed either in Gurdjieff's own writings, or in books about Gurdjieff. It is worth noting however that in the various prospectuses of his Institutes, the training of the will was always included. It is only the method that remains undisclosed.[26]

With this in mind, it is startling to picture Tolson passing this concept on to his students, and it is even more likely that Tolson used the "undisclosed" methods that Gurdjieff taught to train the wills of his championship debate team. Joy Flasch's study documents the profound effect that he had on his academic and domestic associates.

Gurdjieff emphasized that to have one's own "I" and free "will" is a great achievement and even those who desire it sincerely may fail to reach it.[27] The centrality of this idea to Gurdjieff's system is reflected in Tolson's concern with it; in all of Tolson's "difficult" poems the central figures — Herodotus, the Curator, and the speakers of the *Libretto* and "E.&.O.E." — each wrestles with the problem of attaining a unified "I."

IV.

He who destroys illusions in himself and others is punished by the ultimate tyrant, Nature.

Friedrich Nietzsche

The problem that Tolson has presented to students is that they have never had to read it in the way he requires. He was, of course, influenced greatly by Modernism and the example of Eliot and Pound, but his difficulties are not those of Modernism. The difficulties of the modernist poets in New York — Wallace Stevens, E.E. Cummings, Hart Crane, and Marianne Moore — were those of a refusal to be "poetical" in the old sense.[28] George Steiner has called these "ontological" difficulties. The New York modernists were pleased when they achieved "explicit ambiguity" as they had no system behind their verses. Although Crane sought to write a poetry that fit Gurdjieff's system into it, he was too committed to the mode of the *Voyou*, the poet of the unconscious, to find a means for writing "objective poetry," the true poetry of revelation. Tolson's problem was to find a means for using modern poetry to express the teachings that Gurdjieff brought to America.

The problem of communicating the ancient laws of the esoteric system to modern Americans was also a major stumbling block for Gurdjieff. The esoteric system had always been recorded by means of codes and symbols, but these ancient means needed to be updated. After trying to set up his institute and failing, Gurdjieff resorted to writing a series of books; the most interesting work in this series is a 1200-page "science-fiction" satire that was titled *An Objectively Impartial Criticism of the Life of Man* or *Beelzebub's Tales to His Grandson*. The book was deliberately written so as to obscure the meanings. Gurdjieff insisted that the work had to be read three times, and J.G. Bennett states that "Only someone familiar with his ideas and prepared to devote a lot of time and hard study to the chapter[s] could make anything of it." Bennett gives Gurdjieff's motives:

> [Bennett is quoting Paul Anderson] It became evident to us all that *Beelzebub* was the one significant document. All his secrets — or at least all of those that he felt free to reveal — were preserved in *Beelzebub's Tales*, and the task that remained was to prepare people who would be capable of interpreting them. If *Beelzebub's Tales* were a legominism, he needed to teach initiates who could transmit the practical methods which the *Third Series* had been intended to indicate but not to teach.[29]

"Legominism" was Gurdjieff's neologism for a text with a hidden teaching. Only an initiate is properly able to read a legominism. According to Bennett, "The personages of *Beelzebub's Tales* are all images that show us some aspect of human or even superhuman nature."[30] Gurdjieff created his legominisms by using a vocabulary of his own making for most of the important terms: trogoautegocrat, heptaparaparshinokh, triamazikamno, handledzoin, and of course legominism. He employed other techniques as well:

> The apparently slipshod use of words extended into general terms. He would reify abstractions, use concrete expressions in an abstract sense, personify laws and principles. This requires that in reading him, one should set oneself to seize the intention and substance, which calls for a considerable change from our usual

ways of reading. It is hardest of all for professional philosophers and students of language.[31]

Wilburn Williams, Jr., has shown how Tolson altered early versions of lines in *Harlem Gallery* to make them less accessible in the published poem.[32] Tolson realized the difficulties that he was making for his readers, and he refers to this several times in *Harlem Gallery*. In "DELTA" he says:

> Art / leaves her lover as a Komitas / deciphering
> intricate Armenian neums, / with a wild surmise.

Tolson filled his poetry with material from Ouspensky's books, and from the lectures of Thurman, Toomer, and Gurdjieff. It would require a book-length study to show the ways in which he utilized the material.

One of Tolson's favorite techniques is the subject rhyme. He enjoyed finding metonymies and allowing the reader to deduce from the many allusions that the common element was important. In his poem "The Man from Halicarnassus" he has Herodotus say:

> and if the tongue of tongues should die,
> tomorrow's tomorrows will do
> what I have done to yesterdays in Cabiri.[33]

Tolson's difficulties send the reader not to dictionaries, atlases, and encyclopedias (as Dudley Randall and others have asserted) but to primary texts, as do the notes in Eliot's "Waste Land." The reader must not look up Cabiri to find out what is intended here, but must consult Herodotus' *Clio*, where this passage is located:

> Anyone will know what I mean if he is familiar with the mysteries of the Cabiri — rites which the men of Samothrace learned from the Pelasgians, who lived in that island before they moved to Attica, and communicated the mysteries to the Athenians. This will show that the Athenians were the first Greeks to make statues of Hermes with the erect phallus, and that they learned the practice from the Pelasgians — who explained it by a certain religious doctrine, the nature of which is made clear in the Samothracian mysteries.[34]

Allusions in *Libretto* and *The Harlem Gallery* send the reader to similar passages in Jonathan Swift's *Journal to Stella* and to Aeschylus' *Agamemnon*. In Swift the line reads "Ppt (poppet) may understand me." In Aeschylus' play, a nightwatch says:

may it only happen. May my king
come
   home, and I
take up within his hand the hand
   I love. The rest
I leave to silence; for an ox
   stands huge upon my tongue,
The house, itself, could it take voice,
   might speak
aloud and plain. I speak to those
   who understand,
but if they fail, I have forgotten
   everything.

The Swift allusion in *Libretto* is even aided by a note which sends the reader to Swift's journal. There are several allusions to Aeschylus' line in *Harlem Gallery*, for example, "the black ox treads the wine press of Harlem," and "The artist / is / a zinnia / no first frost / blackens with the cloven hoof." The allusion was evidently a favorite; he uses it in "The Man From Halicarnassus" too: "I am no ox-hoof treading ugh upon a scroll." These allusions share the theme of secret knowledge.

Tolson makes things difficult for the reader in that he provides notes that do not help explicate the poem. The notes to *Libretto for the Republic of Liberia* mention books which in turn must be entirely read in order to get at Tolson's meaning. With Tolson, as with Eliot, "a quotation is rarely, perhaps never, only a quotation. It is a doorway into the world of possibilities, feelings, concepts, out of which the quotation, and the whole work to which it belongs, have grown."[35] *Harlem Gallery* was published without notes, however, so one must depend upon the lines to ascertain which books are indicated. In the second stanza of "BETA" the Curator says:

   as the telescope of Galileo
deserted the clod to read the engirdling idioms of
   the star,
     to the ape of God,
       go!

Here, what sounds like rhetoric is meant literally: *The Apes of God* is a novel by Windham Lewis and reading the novel clears up several of the major ambiguities in *Harlem Gallery*. Tolson inserted the phrase "ape of god" at several places in the poem, and it is likely that any repetition of this sort indicates that the phrase has a double meaning.

In *Harlem Gallery, Book I: The Curator*, the narrator has no name. Tolson himself states so as well:

> The Curator is of Afroirishjewish ancestry. He is an octoroon, who is a Negro in New York and a white man in Mississippi. Like Walter White, the late executive of the NAACP, and the author of *A Man Called White*, the Curator is a "voluntary" Negro. Hundreds of thousands of Octoroons like him have vanished in the Caucasian race — never to return. This is a great joke among Negroes. So Negroes ask the rhetorical question, "What man is white?" We never know the real name of the Curator. The Curator is both psychologically and physiologically "the Invisible Man." He as well as his darker brothers think in Negro. Book One is his autobiography. He is a cosmopolite, a humanist, a connoisseur of the fine arts, with catholicity of taste and interest. He knows intimately lowbrows and middlebrows and highbrows.[36]

Published in 1930, Wyndham Lewis' novel *The Apes of God* has as its central character Horace Zagreus. The protagonist, in the course of the novel, is identified as an albino Negro who is also a homosexual and also "sterile." What Tolson has done in *Harlem Gallery* is borrow Horace Zagreus for his own creation. He places the Curator in a Harlem setting a few years after the persona's appearance in Lewis' novel. It is also noteworthy that *The Apes of God*, a satire which ridicules the artists of Bloomsbury, has many similarities to Thurman's *Infants of the Spring*.

In *The Apes of God*, Horace Zagreus is a follower of Pierpoint, Wyndham Lewis' mouthpiece, who is revealed largely through an extract from "The Encyclical," which is a treatise on the unpromising conditions under which true artists practice. Long sections of Pierpoint's encyclical are paraphrased by the Curator in "PI." Pierpoint never appears in *The Apes of God*, but the Curator is paired with Dr. Obi Nkomo in *Harlem Gallery*, leading one to suspect that Nkomo is meant to be thought of as Pierpoint. If we read into Tolson's borrowings and add what we know about the Harlem Group to this exercise, it is clear that Tolson's Curator is based on Jean Toomer, while the absent Pierpoint, revealed as Dr. Nkomo, is Tolson's depiction of G.I. Gurdjieff. Gurdjieff did visit New York in 1924, and he did employ disguises, but his actual appearance as an African in Harlem seems to be more of a joke (though admittedly esoteric) than an actuality. Despite the seeming complexities of these allusions, it is in no way stretching things to try to see Nkomo/Pierpoint as Gurdjieff. In *Apes* Pierpoint is "the apotheosis of the outsider, who can stand back and see things as they really are — 'one of the only people who see,'"[37] while Nkomo has generally been interpreted as a profound thinker whose role in the poem is the reeducation of the misguidedly elitist Curator.

Although this point requires further investigation, it seems that Tolson also borrowed some other elements of *The Apes of God*, for Lewis' novel has been described as a "satire-collage" by Frederic Jameson ("The satire-collage is the form taken by artificial epic in the degraded world of commodity production and of the mass media . . ."), and *Harlem Gallery* is certainly a satire-collage.[38]

A similar complex chain of allusions runs from the title of Sienkiwicz's novel *Quo Vadis* in "UPSILON."

> The Curator and Doctor Nkomo
>   sat staring into space,
>   united like the siphons of a Dosinia —
> the oddest hipsters on the new horizon of Harlem,
>   odder
>   (by odds)
>   than that
>   cabala of a funeral parlor
>   in Cuernavaca,
>   Mexico
>   . . . called . . .
>   "Quo Vadis."

This chain of allusions develops the theme of the ending of an era and the beginning of a new age — in *Quo Vadis* it is the end of Rome, the empire, and in Eliot and Tolson the scene is the decline of the West. Petronius, the Arbiter, is a major character in *Quo Vadis*. The historical Petronius wrote *Satyricon*, another link in Tolson's chain of allusions.

There are many indirect references to scenes in the *Satyricon* in *Harlem Gallery*, and it is interesting to note that Petronius' satire features as its hero Encolpius, an aesthete similar in type to the Curator (and Horace Zagreus). Encolpius is a disreputable poet who is comparable to Tolson's Hideho Heights.

Finally, there is the difficulty of Tolson's use of the esoteric body of knowledge for the subject matter of his poems. Since this information is either kept a close secret or revealed only partially, it is simply not common knowledge. Recently books have been published on Gurdjieff's system, so it is possible to learn the rudiments of the ideas that Tolson used. Here, at least, the difficulties are contingent. Once the reader has been aimed in the direction of occult knowledge, difficulties can be overcome by consulting the proper occult sources. Thus the *Libretto* is understood to be a mystery play in the manner of the hieratic plays of the Great Mysteries of Epoptism wherein mysteries are revealed to initiates. By using the term libretto, Tolson suggests that the poem is an *opera*, which is Latin for "work" — the term both for a magical rite and for Gurdjieff's system. The poem's protagonist is the initiate.

The structure of the *Libretto* — a section for each note in the musical scale — turns out to be a poetic use of one of Gurdjieff's esoteric Great Laws, the cosmic law of seven-foldness, which is symbolized as a musical scale throughout the writings of Ouspensky. Tolson used this particular law, which explains how the world works, to analyze the past and future of Liberia. Tolson referred to this law in his poetry several times as "Do-to-Do" and was constantly finding ways to reveal the action of this law in his poetry. Tolson deepened the imagery of the law of seven-foldness or, as Gurdjieff called it, "three octaves of radiation" by superimposing the first eight-trumps of the Tarot deck over the musical scale: each section of the *Libretto* describes the scene pictured on a Tarot card as the deck is described in Ouspensky's *A New Model of the Universe*. So careful was Tolson to include esoteric material into his poems that he went so far as to provide a numerological element; the 770 lines of the *Libretto* can be interpreted as $770 = 7 \times 10 \times 11$, which is easily read by a student of the Tarot by referring to the cards numbered 7, 10, and 11 — the numbers symbolize the theme of the poem on Liberia's history. Tolson used the word "cabala" in *Harlem Gallery, Libretto*, and "The Man from Halicarnassus." He intended his poetry to yield the secrets only when approached as a text that could reveal the great laws of hermetic occultism. The Curator asks in "OMEGA" (*Harlem Gallery*):

> Do not scholars tear their beards — vex
> their disciples over the Palestinian and Byzantine
> punctuation of the Masoretic texts?

Tolson's poetry best exemplifies objective literature produced by a modernist writer. Although literature is often equated with self-expression, a less recognized strain of modernism descends from the occultist poetry of Rimbaud and Mallarmé, who attempted to write *Le "Livre"* and failed. It was to have been the ideal work of art, the embodiment of an ideal reality. Tolson alludes to Mallarmé's unfinished work in *Harlem Gallery*, and Tolson's later poetry attempts to fulfill the dictates of an ideal art form. It marks an effort to be play, symphony, ballet, song, poem, theatre, hymn, opera.[39] Gurdjieff taught that "The worst thing is to express self, which of course everyone wishes to do. This is why subjective art is a maleficent factor in formation of a soul [sic]."[40] According to the view, self-expression would be denied to Hart Crane, Wallace Thurman, and Jean Toomer, who all desired to create works of objective art — the art of the Superman — the whole purpose of esoteric occultism. While Tolson did not live to carry out his plan for writing a five-volume *Harlem Gallery*, his poetry expresses more absolute laws that that of the other poets mentioned. Tolson often alludes to the esoteric formula that was traditional: "The initiates know what I mean," and also to its admonitory form, "Do not give what is sacred to the dogs." (See *Harlem Gallery*, DELTA for an example of Tolson's use of "the dog.") While an objective artwork does not reveal the meanings to the "dogs," it faithfully records the laws of nature. It must necessarily be difficult, but once the difficulties have been passed, it externalizes and "objectifies" the consciousness of the artist.

Jean Toomer, echoing Aristotle, asserted that "Great art, I was convinced, could issue only from great human beings. Small men could not reproduce really big books."[41] In *Harlem Gallery* Tolson has Doctor Obi Nkomo say: "Life and art beget incestuously." Ultimately, the difficulties of objective poetry are those of consciousness, for as with the study of Cabala, looking things up leads to "ever more radical modifications of consciousness and cognition."[42] Tolson intended for his poetry to be a means whereby "dogs" became Cosmic Individuals. He learned from Toomer that the formation of this new race — into which the Negro would perhaps dubiously disappear forever — was not an automatic process, as some thinkers avowed (Blavatsky and Wyndham Lewis). The voluntary nature of evolution was Tolson's great theme as in *Harlem Gallery*'s last lines:

> Our public may possess in Art
> a Mantegna figure's arctic rigidity;
> yet — I hazard — yet,

> this allegro of the Harlem Gallery
> is not a chippy fire,
> for here, in focus, are paintings that chronicle
> a people's New World odyssey
> from chattel to Esquire!

and in the last line of "The Man From Halicarnassus":

> and mused: "A people can be bat serpents flying
> black abises dying,
> or gods outwearing
> Calpe and Abila, tearing
> Ne plus ultra asunder!"

Work was required to raise the consciousness of Americans, or the chance for Cosmic Manhood would be lost.

NOTES

1. George Steiner, *On Difficulty* (New York: Oxford Univ. Press, 1978), 19.
2. Ibid., 19–20.
3. Dudley Randall, "The Black Aesthetic in the Thirties, Forties, and Fifties," *The Black Aesthetic*, ed. Addison Gayle, Jr. (Garden City, N.Y.: Doubleday, 1971), 218.
4. Eugene B. Redmond, *Drumvoices* (Garden City, N.Y.: Doubleday, 1976), 254.
5. Ibid., 254.
6. Wilburn Williams, Jr., *The Desolate Servitude of Language: A Reading of the Poetry of Melvin B. Tolson* (Ann Arbor, Mich.: University Microfilms, 1983), 182.
7. Ibid., 289. See also Sarah Webster Fabio, "Who Speaks Negro?" *Black Expression*, ed. Addison Gayle, Jr. (New York: Weybright and Talley, 1969), 115–22.
8. Williams, *Desolate Servitude*, 278.
9. Steiner, *On Difficulty*, 40–41.
10. Joy Flasch, *Melvin B. Tolson* (New York: Twayne, 1972), 29.
11. Williams, *Desolate Servitude*, ii.
12. Wallace Thurman, *Infants of the Spring* (New York: Macaulay, 1932), 36.
13. Ibid., 221.
14. Ibid., 218–21.
15. *The Wayward and the Seeking: A Collection of Writings by Jean*

Toomer, ed. Darwin T. Turner (Washington, D.C.: Howard Univ. Press, 1980), 18.

16. Brian J. Benson and Mabel Mayle Dillard, *Jean Toomer* (Boston: Twayne, 1980), 143, quoting Robert Bone.

17. Richard Bruce, "Smoke, Lillies and Jade," *Voices from the Harlem Renaissance*, ed. Nathan I. Huggins (New York: Oxford Univ. Press, 1976), 101.

18. Jean Toomer, *Cane*, ed. Darwin T. Turner (New York: Liveright, 1975), xxiii.

19. Ibid., xxiii.

20. Ibid.

21. Benson and Dillard, 37.

22. Ibid., 37.

23. Melvin B. Tolson, "News Notes [on 'E.&O.E.']," *Poetry*, 78 (Sept. 1951), 369.

24. Melvin B. Tolson, *A Gallery of Harlem Portraits*, ed. Robert M. Farnsworth (Columbia: Univ. of Missouri Press, 1979), 271 (Afterword). Quotations by permission of the Univ. of Missouri Press; Copyright 1979 by the Curators of the Univ. of Missouri.

25. Flasch, *Tolson*, 37.

26. J.G. Bennett, *Gurdjieff: Making A New World* (London: Harper and Row, 1973), 249.

27. Ibid., 249.

28. Eric Homberger, "Chicago and New York: Two Versions of American Modernism," *Modernism 1890–1930*, ed. M. Bradbury and J. McFarlane (Atlantic Highlands, N.J.: Pelican, 1978), 158.

29. Bennett, *Gurdjieff* 176–77, 180.

30. Ibid., 276.

31. Ibid., 276–77.

32. Williams, *Desolate Servitude*, 186.

33. Melvin B. Tolson, "The Man from Halicarnassus," *Poetry*, 81 (Oct. 1952), 75–77.

34. Herodotus, *The Histories*, trans. Aubrey de Selincourt, revised by A.R. Burn (Harmondsworth, Middlesex, England: Penguin, 1973), I, 150; Bk. II, 51.

35. Helen H. Bacon, "The Sibyl in the Bottle," *The Virginia Quarterly Review*, 34, no. 2 (Spring 1858), 262.

36. *A Gallery of Harlem Portraits*, 260.

37. Robert T. Chapman, "Satire and Aesthetics in Wyndham Lewis' *Apes of God*," *Contemporary Literature*, 12, no. 2 (1971), 140.

38. Frederic Jameson, *Fables of Aggression* (Berkeley: Univ. of California Press, 1979), 80.

39. Paula G. Lewis, *The Aesthetics of Stéphane Mallarmé in Relation to His Public* (Cranbury, N.J.: Farleigh Dickinson, 1976), 94.

40. Mme. Harkounian, *Secret Talks With Mr. G.* (Nevada City, Calif.: IDHHB, 1978), 132.

41. Turner (ed.), *The Wayward*, 128.

42. Michael Baigent, *Holy Blood, Holy Grail* (New York: Dell, 1983), 304.

Fred Fetrow

Portraits and Personae:
Characterization in the Poetry of Robert Hayden

Because Robert Hayden often professed an intense interest in people as unique individuals, one is not surprised to find that interest so widely demonstrated and profoundly articulated in his poetry. Similarly, one would expect scrutiny of the methods and results of Hayden's poetic characterization to reveal something about the poet himself. Such revelation, however, ultimately transcends the time-worn notion that an artist's soul can be discerned in his art, because in the particular case of Robert Hayden there is in operation an ironic form of justice that is quite literally poetic. Hayden, who was neglected as a poet of importance for much of his long career, lives on, subliminally incorporated into a vast array of diverse characters. Viewed from the perspective of character study, Hayden's canon forms a composite portrait of its creator; without conscious design the poet indirectly profiled his own traits, views, and values in the depiction of those types and personages which most intrigued him. Further, although Hayden was artfully reticent about speaking out in a lyric confessional voice, he did provide autobiographical revelation through the use of several various personae. Examination of these portraits adds significantly to the profile of the portrayer. So a study of Hayden's characterization offers a two-fold reward: it enhances our appreciation of this poet's ability to bring to life a veritable pantheon of striking personages — real and imagined, historical and fictional, noble and notorious — and such study extends our understanding of the mind and heart of a neglected yet transcendent artist.

Rightly or wrongly, Robert Hayden was and probably continues to be regarded as a poet almost preoccupied with the past, one who took a special interest in Black history in particular. His extensive collection of Black history poems seems to substantiate this image. When critically examined, however, those "history" poems, while constituting a subset of character studies, more accurately manifest themselves as repositories of themes with timeless application and universal concern. The historical portraits themselves can be further subdivided into two categories, each category with a thematic unity running through the variations of context and personality. One set consists of "real" people who shared the uncommon common goals of freedom and truth. Hayden's set of "freedom fighters" includes obscure leaders of slave revolts early in the nation's history, the famous and infamous from the Civil War era (Frederick Douglass, John Brown) as well as modern Black activists such as Malcolm X. Other portraits in a similar mode of historical personages treated as racial heroes share the role of inspirer—artists and entertainers who function as "light bringers," providing example or escape to help an oppressed people cope. These figures range from Phillis Wheatley to Bessie Smith to Paul Robeson. Aside from the critical assessment of Hayden's narrative virtuosity in such portraits, one can learn much by considering how and why this poet resurrects these particular people from the pages and footnotes of history.

This sort of consideration is often comparative, as a reader checks Hayden's portrayal against the truth or myth of documented and received historical knowledge of these figures. Perhaps more intriguing are Hayden's totally imaginative characters, partially because of an absence of external historical context. One must measure such characters with cultural markers and bring to bear one's own assumptions about human nature and personal psychology. Many of these people are what Hayden liked to call "folk characters," examples or composites of people he had observed in his life or imagined in his retrospective view of human behavior. While some "types" are culturally recognizable, all are individually unique and psychologically plausible. In mode these portraits vary from image sketches to symbolic exampla, and many poems are dramatic monologues of self-revelation, revealing both the psyche of the poetic subject and the emotional priorities of the poet. Thus even the study of purely fictional characters adds to the portrait of Robert Hayden.

The third set of characters brings us closer to Hayden himself, albeit in "disguise" as personae not necessarily limited to the poet's identity. That is, these characters suggest many aspects of Hayden's life and person, but they also accommodate more inclusive readings. When augmented by the portrait collection in Hayden's "family album," those poems in portrayal of his ancestry, relatives, and immediate family members, the several "anonymous" personae provide deeply personal psychological insights into Robert Hayden the man. That such revelatory poems increased in number and degree of exposure relatively late in Hayden's life and career now seems ironically appropriate. The poet who even then guardedly revealed himself to his readers wanted his poetry to come first.[1] Only with a fuller knowledge and deeper appreciation of his work could Hayden comfortably seek a sympathetic personal understanding from a belatedly forming audience. This study aims toward such a conjunction, where after seeing the poet's subconscious embodiment of himself in his created characters and his deliberately crafted disguises of himself in others, readers may not only extend their critical understanding of Hayden's artistry, but also gain a better sense of Hayden himself. To that end this brief survey is conceived as a tentative addition to Hayden's gallery of portraits — a critical rather than creative sketch of the poet, with his work in poetic characterization as the medium through which the artist emerges.

Ironically, Robert Hayden's extensive knowledge of Black history derived indirectly from economic disadvantage. As the Great Depression exacerbated the poverty he shared with other Detroit ghetto dwellers, the young man left college and "graduated" to government-sponsored employment with the WPA Federal Writers' Project in 1936. The aspiring poet was assigned to research the history of abolition movements and Underground Railroad activity in Michigan during the Civil War era. His findings and subsequent independent research quite naturally found their way into his *real* work: the poetry he conceived as providing a Black perspective on neglected elements of American history.

An early example typifies Hayden's interests, as well as his "trial flight" status as a novice chronicler of cultural history. His first poem about Crispus Attucks, "Whereas in Freedom's Name . . . ," contrasts sharply in poetic mode and thematic implication with Hayden's 1975 profile of this Black Revolutionary War martyr.[2] A comparative glance proves illuminating. In the early poem Hayden presents Attucks in a linear fashion, where repeated references to his physical height ("tall," "giant," "tallest") serve to allegorize the character as a representative symbol of the revolutionary spirit. Beyond this straightforward patriotic analogy, Hayden also posits an unrecognized "larger meaning" for Attucks' significance as a "type" who epitomizes the progression from slave to fugitive to manhood. When readdressing the same subject over thirty years later, the poet adopts a deliberately ironic and ambiguous perspective. This mature treatment accomplishes a superb merger of form and function. Within the brief span of this four-line poem Hayden visually reinforces the notion of neglected Black heroism by reducing Attucks to a "Name in a footnote. Faceless name" even as he extends the poem's implications with imagery and allusion. Evoking the familiar 1770 engraving by Paul Revere of the Boston Massacre, Hayden portrays Attucks "propped up / by bayonets, forever falling."[3] More significantly, this "moot hero" is "shrouded in Betsy Ross / and Garvey flags," thus both obscured and mantled by the contrary forces of traditional white patriotism and thwarted Black nationalism. In effect, Hayden, within the symbolic figure of Crispus Attucks, distills American history into paradox and then impels it into the present by making his portrait of Attucks as immutable as any of the figures on Keats's famous urn. As rendered by Hayden, Attucks remains eternally in pursuit of a freedom eternally elusive; by implication the progression from "manhood" to truth continues.

The pursuit of truth also informs Hayden's characterization of other Black heroes who rebelled against the society for which Crispus Attucks died. As early as in his first published collection of poems, Hayden attempted to give voice and presence to Gabriel Prosser, who led an ill-fated slave revolt in Virginia during 1800.[4] Although this portrait shares a similarity in visionary premise with Hayden's later portrayal of Nat Turner, "Gabriel" is cast in a dialogue format to allow the subject to answer questions as he prepares to face execution. In expressing his views the character functions as a voice of prophecy, but he is more voice than person, his "prophecy" little more than a final wish. One can intellectually envision Gabriel as "a sword in the air" whose "spirit goes flying / Over the land / With a song in his mouth / And a sword in his hand," but Prosser as a moral spokesman never achieves the dimensions of character needed to validate his spiritual influence.

By contrast, Hayden's portrait of Nat Turner is a masterpiece of psychological characterization.[5] The poet's own testimony clarifies his priorities: "As I studied the accounts of the rebellion, what interested me was not the bloodshed but Nat Turner himself, his characteristics, his personality. . . . Turner's essentially mysterious qualities greatly stimulated my imagination."[6] The result is "The Ballad of Nat Turner," wherein Hayden imaginatively projects Turner as a religious zealot whose fanatical faith manifests itself as an obsession with freedom obtained through God-endorsed violence. He conveys aspects of Turner's personality by using a dramatic monologue in which Turner describes his visions to an imagined audience of Black followers. As Hayden explains, "By having him speak, I thought I could reveal him more dramatically and with greater economy. I could create a stronger illusion of a living presence."[7] Through Turner's description of his visions, Hayden achieves a humanizing balance in characterization between the essential traits of mysterious charisma and fearful vulnerability. Thus does Hayden's version of Nat Turner come to life with more credible personality and motivation than the psychological cripple created by William Styron or the equally fictitious, idealized revolutionary preferred by some Black historians and scholars.[8] Moreover, Hayden wisely establishes a situational context to present Turner before the 1831 slave revolt but after his several mystical experiences. Thereby the poet assures concentration on character with no distraction from the rebellion itself or the repercussions that followed.

Yet another leader of slave rebellion stirred Hayden's interest and imagination during the early stages of his poetic evolution. The handling of the character called "Cinque" in his masterly poem, "Middle Passage," shares with the original Attucks portrait the conception of a single symbolic character who embodies the determined struggle for freedom by an entire race. Through deft use of a montage of narrative voices, Hayden transcends either strict historical documentation or limited racial utterance. Indeed, the character Hayden would have readers accept as a "deathless primaveral image" speaks not at all in the poem. Instead, the poet daringly characterizes Cinque through the condemnation of a Spanish prosecution witness at the "Amistaders'" trial.[9] When considered within the larger framework of the poem's narrative materials and the situational irony laid like a trap by Hayden, this hostile witness unknowingly damns himself and edifies Cinque. For example, in arrogantly rationalizing having been overcome by inferior "apes," the Spaniard repeatedly refers to the adverse weather conditions which lowered their guard and weakened their defenses against the slaves. His conclusion that the slave attack "was as though the very / air, the night itself were striking us" ironically implies that Nature itself assisted the cause of freedom. The ultimate effect of such "negative" characterization is the emergence of Cinque as a figure of heroic stature. As prepared for and borne out by the other narrative segments of "Middle Passage," Cinque evolves into a symbolic personification of the universally human aspiration for personal liberty. Hayden, in the voice of a central moral narrator, calls this urge "the deep immortal human wish, / the timeless will," and Hayden as poet convincingly postulates Cinque as the "deathless primaveral image" of that will, as a "life that transfigures many lives."

The indirection of Cinque's characterization perhaps derives from Hayden's thematic design, but this oblique view also enhances the sense of a mysterious hero with some sort of spiritual assistance if not divine ordination. In that sense Cinque exerts the spiritual force that Gabriel Prosser prophesies as a dying wish and that Nat Turner visualizes in his religious mania. But in "Middle Passage" it is the indomitable will of humankind which the poet celebrates; the spiritual force manifested by Nature remains secondary. Robert Hayden's view of the natural world in the early 1940s is thus spiritually "glossed" but seemingly in ambivalent terms. Perhaps as he shrank away from the influences of a fundamentalist religious upbringing and edged toward his adoption of the Bahái faith in 1942, he found less solace in doctrine and more faith in humanity.[10]

Certainly Hayden's time-lapse view of John Brown reflects such a shift. He first wrote in depiction of Brown in "Fire Image," which helped form the sheaf of poems that won for Hayden the Hopwood Major Award in Poetry in 1942.[11] As the poem's title suggests, Hayden sketches Brown as a God-chosen agent of truth, one fated to "burn in swift and javelined flight." The younger Hayden perhaps overburdens the central metaphoric tenor as he variously equates fire with anger, truth, and revelation and acknowledges that Brown was both "profoundly loved and hated / because his blistering gaze is Truth." Essentially, Hayden views this controversial figure through the "sleepless eyes" of oppressed Blacks, "who, hidden, wait" and watch Brown burning like a torch in their behalf. Hayden closes the poem with a pointed allusion to the phoenix myth, claiming that Brown's "ashes flower / to myth and blinding prophecy." In spite of copious imagery (or perhaps because of it), the poem is so laden with message that John Brown as a man or even as a character does not really inhabit the verse. Hayden seems so blinded by the light of his fire images that he cannot see the man behind them.

When Hayden was commissioned in 1978 by the Detroit Institute of Arts to write a poem about John Brown to accompany Jacob Lawrence's paintings of the same subject, the poet determined to do justice to Brown, Lawrence, and himself. With "John Brown" he certainly does.[12] He adds and incorporates Brown's voice and psyche, thereby heightening and making central the ambivalence only hinted at in the 1942 version's love-hate response to Brown's activities. "Fire image" is not a bad poem; it is simply more image than theme, and more theme than characterization; whereas "John Brown" integrates all of these elements, including Black, white and transcendently non-racial perspectives on Brown's significance.

These variants in perspective stem from a modal texture of mixed narrative voices. Among them, Brown himself speaks in defensive rationalization of his deeds. An external narrator subsequently ponders this "Fury of truth; fury / of righteousness," questioning whether Brown has "become angelic evil" or "demonic good." That Hayden consciously consulted his earlier poem in qualifying his certainty about Brown is clearly evidenced in the correlation of recurring diction and altered phrasing. In the former poem Hayden depicts his subject "in splendid anger aureoled," but in "John Brown" he is "aureoled in violence." In the first version Hayden identifies Brown as one "whose soul became / the body of Jahveh's kindled wrath," but by the second version the divine ordainment premise has been reduced to a questionable possibility. Seemingly, Hayden's mature view became as ambivalent as the historical context may have originally suggested. Although the narrator again asks, "Who sent you here, John Brown?" he also regards Brown a successor to "Gabriel and Nat" who are "awaiting him." Hayden once more conclusively views John Brown from a Black perspective, sharpening the focus without altering the ambiguity. He claims that Brown's sacrifice for the cause of Black liberty ("Shall we not say he died for us?") is all we know and all we need to know. Finally, in regard of the original artistic setting of "John Brown," Hayden directs the reader's attention toward Lawrence's paintings with reference to the "mordant images . . . in ardent interplay / with what we know of him / know yet fail to understand —."

Hayden immortalizes another abolitionist with his own unique form of poetic prophecy. His tribute to the memory of Frederick Douglass takes the shape of the highly innovative sonnet first published in 1947.[13] Rather than treating his subject through biographical sketch or personality profile, Hayden concentrates on a conceptual linkage between human freedom and Douglass' legacy. Utilizing a lengthy periodic sentence, he first defines "freedom" variously but methodically, delineating a progression from freedom as an abstract idea to freedom as a concrete, living reality. The poet takes a considerable rhetorical risk in bringing "freedom" into sharp clarity and then asserting unequivocally that when such complete freedom is fully realized, Frederick Douglass will be "remembered" and thus immortalized "with the lives grown out of his life, the lives / fleshing his dream of the beautiful, needful thing."

In fact, Hayden combines paean and protest by concluding the sonnet in a subtle yet striking paradox. Implicitly, he denies the present fulfillment of Douglass' dream by claiming that when total freedom is achieved, Douglass will not be remembered "with legends and poems and wreathes of bronze alone." While his poem celebrates freedom, the very existence of this sort of tribute signals the limitation of freedom because when true freedom "arrives," all such tributes will be superfluous. So "Frederick Douglass" is as much about freedom as it is about the ostensible subject. Hayden does acknowledge history and personality, however, in five of the fourteen lines. He personalizes Douglass as "superb in love and logic," a balance of intellect and compassion. Yet the man's personality is subsumed finally by his legacy; he is the embodiment of a noble concept, and as such he lives on, immortalized in the freedoms enjoyed by his racial and human progeny.

In almost obverse fashion, Hayden profiles Harriet Tubman in terms of tangible deed, her physical activities as a conductor on the Underground Railroad. Significantly, although she is the central dramatic interest in "Runagate Runagate," Hayden introduces her relatively late in the poem.[14] The first section establishes the overall premise of escape from slavery by running away to the North, and provides narrative subsections to emphasize the pervasiveness of such efforts. There Hayden sets in motion the foot-pounding rhythms of escape ("Runagate Runagate Runagate"), and attributes the urge for freedom to an anonymous, representative "everyslave" figure who stands for the masses, and by moral implication, the human spirit. With respect to Tubman's role in the poem, Hayden delays her entry for thematic purposes. Without diminishing her heroic status, he first wants to establish that the aspiration for and pursuit of freedom among enslaved Blacks was the rule and not the exception. Harriet Tubman appears later in the poem to lead, assist, and guide unidentified, composite "runagates," but it is their individual and collective strength of will which makes understandable her heroism. Indeed, Hayden introduces her in Section Two as the product of such qualities; Tubman "Rises from their anguish and their power," a "woman of earth, whipscarred, / a summoning, a shining."

In that section the poet dramatizes this relationship and Tubman's own strengths through an excerpted monologue by another anonymous runagate, who describes his "journey from Can't to Can" on her "ghost-story train." When their determination falters, she physically redoubles hers, as she checks the fears and doubts of her charges with an even more direct threat than possible recapture:

> And she's turned on us, levelled pistol
> glinting in the moonlight:
> Dead folks can't jaybird-talk she says;
> you keep on going now or die, she says.

Hayden fleshes out her persona with other narrative materials, such as facsimile wording from a "wanted" poster advertising reward for Tubman's capture "Dead or Alive." These seemingly "objective" elements lend authenticity to the portrait, while extending its dimensions. The epithets and aliases by which Tubman was known characterize her place in history more than they reveal personal traits, but the contrasts in how she was viewed have the effect of expanding the poem back to its original premise. To white slavers and their sympathizers, Tubman is a "Dangerous" "Stealer of Slaves"; to her followers and supporters she is a liberating "Moses" and "The General." Hayden thus highlights Harriet Tubman's significant role in the Black liberation movement and pays her due homage, but his ultimate thematic emphasis is on the spirit and resolve of the countless "runagate" slaves whom he designates collectively in his title. His repetition of this designator thus quantifies their numbers even as the term echoes the rhythm of their determined movement. Hayden deliberately avoids a personalized or psychological study of Harriet Tubman in order to keep the reader's attention on what one is tempted to call the "critical mass" of a freedom-seeking people.

On the basis of these representative examples of historical figures important to Robert Hayden, one could generalize that while he admired selfless sacrifice and heroic deed, he was most intrigued with those mysterious or obscured personalities who somehow transcended their individuality. Contrarily, almost paradoxically, he seemed urged to ennoble "common" mankind by linking unique heroism to a collective racial or human mass identity. In view of these apparent patterns, it seems almost inevitable that Hayden would write about a modern exhorter of truth and freedom whose personality defied reductive summary, and whose reputation still remains shrouded in mystery and controversy.

His poem about Malcolm X, "El-Hajj Malik El-Shabazz," combines nearly every quality of those character portraits previously examined in these pages.[15] Hayden read *The Autobiography of Malcolm X*, and its influence shows; the poem follows the chronological outline of a biographical sketch, right down to the inclusion of some of Malcolm's nicknames that Alex Haley uses as chapter titles ("Home Boy," "Detroit Red," "Satan").[16] But as employed by Hayden these names figure in a thematic scheme as well; in the poet's perception, Malcolm's life reveals the characteristic features of a classical identity quest, a subconscious search for self that moves the quester through a continuing metamorphosis of character and spiritual experience.

Hayden's opening epigraph suggests his conception of Malcolm X and hints at how the portrait should be viewed: "*O masks and metamorphoses of Ahab, Native Son.*" Without realizing it, Malcolm works his way through several false identities during his life. The "Native Son" phase incorporates the same brutal ironies inherent in Richard Wright's title, where Malcolm, like Bigger Thomas, as the "quarry of / his own obsessed pursuit," is both culprit and victim in a racist society that has created and yet spurned him. In prison he achieves a "false dawn of vision" as he subscribes to the equally racist theology of Elijah Muhammad's Nation of Islam. Newly converted and returned to society, Malcolm exhorts self-pride among his race, as he "X'd his name, became his people's anger." He became "their scourger who / would shame them, drive them from / the lush ice gardens of their servitude." Yet Malcolm combats oppression while wearing the self-deceiving mask of false righteousness; the moral paradox of this false identity was that in "rejecting Ahab, he was of Ahab's tribe." In his hatred of "white-faced treachery," Malcolm, like Melville's obsessed Ahab, himself becomes diabolical in his attack upon the evils besetting his race.

Eventually, as the process of metamorphosis continues, Malcolm strikes through his own mask. The trip to Mecca in 1964 opens his eyes to the raceless brotherhood of the orthodox Islamic faith and changes his "prideful anger" to spiritual transcendence. Hayden calls that fateful trip "the ebb time pilgrimage / toward revelation, hejira to / his final metamorphosis." Transformed by the experience, newly self-identified by his Sunni Muslim name, El-Hajj Malik El-Shabazz returned to America "renewed" and "renamed," where he "became / much more than there was time for him to be." Hayden's poetic portrait, for all its attendance on chronological fact, reads like a spiritual biography. There can be little doubt that Malcolm X came to believe in the spiritual unity of all mankind, and Hayden implies that the martyr would have acted on that faith had he been given the opportunity.[17]

As his interview commentaries suggest, Hayden's interest in Malcolm X was perhaps more personal than poetic. No doubt part of that intensity of feeling had its source in the poet's own experiences in identity crisis. Considering that he was raised from infancy by foster parents who only grudgingly shared his love with his natural mother, who returned to Detroit and lived near (and, for a time, with) the Haydens during Robert's adolescence, it is not surprising that he often spoke of having a "divided self."[18] In a poem called "Names" he recalls his response to the peculiar "midlife crisis" he experienced at age forty when he discovered that in fact his foster parents had never adopted him, that his "real" name was Asa Bundy Sheffey, and that his life-long existence as Robert Hayden had been in effect a colossal oversight, if not slight.[19] Given that background, plus his "displacement" in the South at Fisk University for over twenty years, and his spiritual migration from strict fundamentalism to the Baha'i faith, little wonder Hayden found Malcolm X an intriguing subject worthy of his empathetic understanding.

If Hayden was guided and perhaps constrained by the documented biographical facts in portraying Malcolm X, no such boundaries pertain to his characterization of America's first recognized Black poet. Among the several artists and entertainers whom Robert Hayden resurrected, none is more remote in time and culture than Phillis Wheatley. Her personal traits and even most biographical data have been lost to the past. Because Wheatley's extant *ouvre* reflects little more than the typical neo-classical exclusion of self, Hayden began with only a few remaining Wheatley letters and relied upon his imagination to project what she could have been like. In short, Hayden's Phillis Wheatley belongs as much to him as she does to history. Awareness of this distinction provides some insight into the poet who recreated another poet, because those traits he implicitly attributes to her can be retrospectively discerned in Robert Hayden himself.

Simply titled "A Letter from Phillis Wheatley," the poem is that letter, ostensibly written from London in 1773.[20] Michael Harper called this work a "psychogram"; it is another of Hayden's many variations on the dramatic monologue formula whereby he captures and reflects in cryptic fashion the essential personality of the speaker-subject. He achieves verisimilitude in the style and believability in the content of the letter; while its author seems informal, personal, and almost "chatty," the overall tone is restrained by a carefully wrought eighteenth-century elegance in diction and phrasing. Much of the poem's dramatic tension derives from subtly distinct levels of irony. This discrepancy of perception lends drama to the poem as it unfolds Wheatley's sensibility. Since she perceives one level of irony and seems oblivious to or "above" other ironies *not* lost on the reader, she functions as a sort of nobly "naïve narrator." For example, she notes the ironic contrast between her recent ocean voyage to England and her previous westward crossing in the bonds of slavery, but she senses no similar irony in her unquestioned acceptance of her earlier slave status ("my Destined— / voyage") as God's doing. In reporting her treatment among England's nobility, she wryly perceives their interest in her as a novelty ("I thought of Pocahontas"), but she finds no inconsistency in being lauded by the same aristocrats who exclude her from their table ("I dined apart / like captive Royalty"). While gratified by the attention bestowed upon her, as a true "Patriot," she seems overly concerned about the propriety of being presented at the English court. Ever the staunch Calvinist, even in "Idyllic England" she realizes "there is / no Eden without its Serpent." But her refusal to trouble her friend with a "Sombreness" probably warranted by her circumstance in life leads her to conclude the letter with an anecdote she finds "Droll." She reports an encounter on a London street with a soot-covered young chimney sweep who "politely asked: / 'Does you, M'lady, sweep chimneys too?'" Wheatley's amusement at this innocently ironic event perhaps best summarizes Hayden's conception of her as an imaginary character. He clearly admires her poetic sensibility and devout piety, but he makes most memorable her refreshing ability to appreciate life's lighter ironies. His portrait of Phillis Wheatley bears all the traces of a labor of love; history has neglected her, but Hayden has done art a great service in re-creating her, perhaps subconsciously in his own image.

Robert Hayden's homage to Paul Laurence Dunbar shows a similarly empathetic yet fully conscious identification with his subject. Occasioned by a visit to Dunbar's gravesite in the company of fellow poet, Herbert Martin, "Paul Laurence Dunbar" comes closest to formal elegy of any of Hayden's "remembrances" of historical figures.[21] Adopting a first-person plural voice, Hayden speaks for himself, for Herbert Martin, and for their generation of Black poets when he addresses the occasion in terms of Dunbar's life and work. As they mourn for him "as if he were but newly dead," the spokesman views Dunbar's dialect poetry, those "verses 'in a broken tongue,'" as masked emblems of a broken life. Just as the "sad blackface lilt and croon" of Dunbar's popular poetry were guises of carefree happiness concealing the sorrows of limited lives, so Dunbar's outward success was "subliminal / of victim, dying man." Most poignantly, these verses survive their deceased creator; like a happy expression on a faded photograph, such false gaiety cannot either truly represent its subject or comfort its beholders. Hayden's speaker begins the poem by ceremoniously laying red roses on Dunbar's grave. The formal contemplation concludes on that same note, except that as in the contemplation itself, reality impinges upon the reverie:

> The roses flutter in the wind;
> we weight their stems
> with stones, then drive away.

The roses that do not blow away will soon wither; only the stones will remain.

Hayden characterizes other historical figures from Black culture by portraying them with a collective point-of-view, in the eyes and hearts of those audiences who found solace in their performances. "Homage to the Empress of the Blues," Hayden's remembrance of Bessie Smith, whom he had seen and heard at the Koppin Theater as a young man in Detroit, reflects this pattern of presentation.[22] By alternating his emphasis between Smith's elegant stage presence and those circumstances of Black society which made her music so pertinent to their lives, the poet summarizes this "folk artist" as a benefactress, a momentary "escape" from the fearful realities of oppression, poverty, and violence. Smith's blues songs provided a realism her audiences could identify with out of sweet sorrow rather than downright fear.

Thus the poet's stylized excerpting of some of her popular themes ("Faithless Love / Twotiming Love Oh Love Oh Careless Aggravating Love") contrasts with his description of her stage appearance and her effect upon the audience: "She came out on the stage in yards of pearls, emerging like / a favorite scenic view, flashed her golden smile and sang." Ultimately, Hayden establishes an explicit causal relationship between her glowing performances and their emotional need, saying in effect that because poverty could not be permanently patched over, because people had to live in constant fear of the authority figures of legalized racism (" . . . alarming fists of snow / on the door . . . the riot-squad of statistics"), because these disheartening conditions existed, "She came out on the stage in ostrich feathers, beaded satin, / and shone that smile on us and sang."

Hayden structures the poem to emulate Bessie Smith's actual performances; with the blues-like refrain in varied depiction of her image on stage, preceded and followed by narrative in description of desperate lives, he at once suggests the recurring respite Smith's music afforded and shapes that statement itself in the general form of a blues song, with its repeating pattern of narrative and refrain. In this succinct mode Hayden, speaking for the "people," justly acclaims Bessie Smith a cultural phenomenon even as he characterizes the culture making that claim.

He again links a "hero" to the masses in his erudite recollection of a local prizefighter prominent in the Midwest during the Depression era. Hayden began fascinated by the exotic sound of his name, "Tiger Flowers," and created a character to match.[23] The resultant "Free Fantasia" uses Flowers as a focal point around which Hayden gathers a widely mixed cast of "supporting" characters. This cast runs the social gamut from "the sporting people," who "bet salty money / on his [Flowers'] righteous / hook and jab," to "Creole babies, / Dixie odalisques," who view the boxer as a "macho angel / trick," and even includes "Hardshell believers," who "amen'd" Flowers' victories "as God A'mighty's / will." Through this diversity runs the central theme of vicarious triumph; like Joe Louis on a national scale, Tiger Flowers with his public prowess allows local people to share his victories, to counter the defeats in their own lives.[24] Small wonder then that they consider him "our / elegant avenger."

Hayden's concluding allusion to Henri Rousseau's painting, *The*

Virgin Forest, at first reading seems inappropriate if not pretentious, either as a synopsis of the poem or "as elegy for Tiger Flowers," but a cursory glance at the painting makes understandable Hayden's judicious reference. That impressionistic view of the natural world, with its "psychedelic flowers" as setting for a dominating exotic leopard is well suited to emblematize the exotica Hayden senses in the name "Tiger Flowers," and to suggest the psychic mystery of the inspiration this boxer ("deathless / dark dream figure") gives those who lift themselves up by cheering him on. As with his portrayal of Bessie Smith, Hayden in "Free Fantasia: Tiger Flowers" traces the pattern of an exotic figure lending light to the darkened lives of an oppressed people. This thematic concept is so strong an impulse in Hayden's habits of characterization that one can discern the motif in several of the poet's fictional portraits as well.

In order of composition, Hayden's "Homage to Paul Robeson" is his final poem in characterization or commemoration of a real figure from history.[25] The timing, as well as the poem, is an ironically suitable ending to this phase of the poet's creative activity, because he achieves an ideal balance of thought and feeling in a tribute which could well serve as his own epitaph. To appreciate fully the verity of such generalizations, one must see the work entire:

> Call him deluded, say that he
> was dupe and by half-truths betrayed.
> I speak him fair in death,
> remembering the power of his
> compassionate art. All else fades.

As a portrait sketch of its subject, "Homage" clearly eschews objectivity; Hayden is here more personal, more subjective than usual. But this direct statement of feeling "works" because of its compelling moral priority. Hayden confronts head-on questionable areas of Robeson's reputation without rhetorical disputation; instead he simply dismisses those negative elements as irrelevant to the higher truths of Robeson's life. Compared to the "power of his / compassionate art," all else *does* fade. By reducing this assertion to its marrow, Hayden makes it absolutely convincing.

Ironically (and again, appropriately), this "reduction" to pure feeling is the end product of careful craftsmanship. Hayden first wrote an earlier version almost four times as long, using a reverie premise to recall Robeson's involvement in labor organizing activities in the late 1930s.[26] In the creative process he eventually transported Paul Robeson from Cadillac Square in Detroit to the reader's consciousness by cutting and thereby drastically revising the poem into its final form. He thus caused literally "all else" to fade from his own work, distilling the poem to the final five lines.

One of those lines, in its moral implication and allusive source, indicates Hayden's ultimate objective. "I speak him fair in death" paraphrases a line from Shakespeare's *Merchant of Venice* where Antonio, anticipating his own end, asks Bassanio to commend him to Portia: "Say how I lov'd you, speak me fair . . ." (IV.i.275). In the context of Shakespeare's dramatic situation, the request assumes that survivors can give meaning to the life of one recently dead through the manner in which they report the attributes of the deceased. Such is the case of "Homage," where Hayden recalls Robeson in terms of the legacy of his art, emphasizing equally its power and its compassion. Thus the poet indelibly identifies Paul Robeson with those attributes; and as his poem simultaneously advocates, claims, and artfully proves, "All else fades."

Robert Hayden's own legacy in historical characterization is a similar one. When considering the strikingly unique artistry with which he brings back to life an array of racial, cultural, and national figures, one notes how pervasively the artist merges the heroism of these personages with the strengths and needs of "ordinary" humanity. Even a dispassionately "analytical" critic is compelled to speak Hayden fair, to recognize "the power of his / compassionate art."

Robert Hayden drew many of his fictional characters from observation of real individuals or by assembling composites; he acknowledged such sources in designating some figures as "folk characters." This pattern of composition and the poems themselves suggest again that recurrent bonding between individualized portraits and larger cultural groupings, a correlation which apparently fascinated the poet. Contrarily, he also had a strong interest in particular kinds of individuals who were for various reasons excluded or alienated from society. He was forthright in sharing his views on this peculiar preference:

> I'm more interested in people than in things or abstractions. . . . In heroic and "baroque" people especially; in outsiders, pariahs, losers.[27]

> The dramatic personalities, strong baroque personalities, as I have called them, will often lead me to want to write. . . . There are all

kinds of people, and there are all sorts of dramatic possibilities. Well, for the reasons I have given, there is a kind of mystery — there is something that lies beneath the surface they present. I like to try to find out what it is that gives them their unique and special qualities.[28]

Hayden's predilection for writing individual poems about particular characters manifests itself in his earliest work, although then the dramatic qualities of his mature portraits had yet to evolve. In addition to those sketches of Crispus Attucks and John Brown in his 1940 *Heart-Shape* collection, one portrait in particular augurs the poet's development as a characterist:

> "Old Woman with Violets"
> Quiet and alone she stands
> Within the whirling market-place,
> Holding the spring in winter hands
> and April's shadow in her face.[29]

"Old Woman" in its haiku-like brevity seems scarcely more than a snapshot, but the symbolic implications of this image constitute the mysterious significance in the ordinary which Hayden had already begun to perceive, if not fully articulate.

The full voice of dramatic possibility can be discerned in later portraits such as "Mourning Poem for the Queen of Sunday."[30] Hayden exploits the inherent drama of situation by compounding it in at least three ways: First, he adopts the narrative voice of a "folk character" who speaks for the congregation in their expression of grief. The narrator's sorrow takes the self-contradictory forms of selfish concern for their loss and a kind of morbid curiosity about the Queen's private life. This perspective, of course, intensifies the central dramatic disparity between the singer's inspiring "otherness" as the Lord's "fancy warbler" on Sundays, and the mortalizing possibility of sordidness in her life during the rest of the week. The narrator's refrain,

> Satan sweet-talked her,
> four bullets hushed her.
> Who would have thought
> she'd end that way?

punctuates this disparity throughout the poem. Finally, the format of the work itself creates an implicit dramatic contrast. Like the Bessie Smith portrait, "Mourning Poem" reads like the artistic form as-

sociated with its subject. The structure imitates gospel music in the
several facets of diction, phrasing, rhythms and narrative-choral
refrain. The content of this particular "song," however, sharply di-
verges from the typical gospel hymn message of present hope and
future certainty. Indeed, the narrator's repeated rhetorical question-
ing in the opening half of the poem establishes the mood of anxiety
about the immediate future, a mood apparently prevalent among the
congregation. Their concern is again voiced in the query,

> Oh who and oh who will sing Jesus down
> to help with struggling and doing without and being colored
> all through blue Monday?
> Till way next Sunday?

Through these devices Hayden makes primary the dramatized theme
of "Mourning Poem." The ironic contrast between human nature's
yearning to be uplifted by God's "diva," and yet titillated by her "sins
of the flesh" finally characterizes those "mourners" as certainly as
the poem eulogizes its title character.

Another exploration of what "lies beneath the surface" yields both
a complex outward character and an even more complex psyche. Per-
haps for these reasons "Witch Doctor" has been one of Hayden's least
understood, least appreciated, and yet most artistically successful
works from what he called his "baroque period."[31] This particular
poem has received "pot-shots" from both sides in an ongoing racial-
critical skirmish. David Galler clearly had "Witch Doctor" in mind
when in a superficial review of Hayden's *Selected Poems* he coined
"hyper-erudition" in generalizing that Black poets ". . . are given to
one of two extremes — sentimentality or hyper-erudition. . . . Hayden
is saddled with both."[32] Ironically, LeRoi Jones (Imamu Amiri Ba-
raka) also criticized the poem "because it was full of fancy-pants
words."[33] What too few readers in either camp fully appreciate is the
extent to which Hayden's erudite diction is part of a deliberate, func-
tional, organic design of characterization and theme.

Hayden deliberately loads the narrative with a mind-boggling ar-
ray of esoteric diction to capture and convey the "glittering flourish,"
the "outrageous flair" of an inner-city evangelistic charlatan in
"garments jeweled and chatoyant." As this ostentatiousness suggests,
the "Witch Doctor" is all show with no substance in rational theol-
ogy or personal faith. Yet the "faith" of his followers is as heartfelt
as his is sham. But of course theirs is a totally heartfelt faith, a fervor

bordering on emotional orgy. The witch doctor's ability to create and orchestrate such an emotional pitch among his audience is a measure of his showmanship and deceptive artistry.

In fact, the casual reader could become so "enmeshed" in the diction of Hayden's narrative that he could overlook perhaps the most telling sign of the poet's functional use of language in this baroque mode. First, note the language of the only sustained speech by a character in the poem. Hayden introduces the witch doctor's mother, his "priestess in gold lamé," in the second stanza, and gives her lines to introduce her son to his audience. Her street dialect and homely metaphors vividly contrast with the baroque language preceding and following, as she "Shouts in blues-contralto,"

> He's
> God's dictaphone of all-redeeming truth.
> Oh he's the holyweight champeen who's come
> to give the knockout lick to your bad luck;
> says he's the holyweight champeen who's here
> to deal a knockout punch to your hard luck.

But when he finally does appear, he only appears. Notice that except for his brief mock opening prayer, the witch doctor never utters a single decipherable word. He "sways, quivers, gesticulates"; he "utters wildering vocables, / hypnotic no-words"; he "chants and trembles"; but never does his "sermon" articulate anything other than emotion. His followers respond in kind:

> Disheveled antiphons proclaim the moment
> his followers all day have hungered for,
> but which is his alone.

The inattentive reader may be similarly "excluded," in that the deliberate distraction of baroque language may cause one to overlook that verbal void filled only by empty gestures. If so, that reader would miss the full extent of the witch doctor's deception (and of Hayden's artistry) because he would see only the words in the poem and not "hear" the silence. No wonder some readers have belittled the poem as "hyper-erudition" or "fancy-pants words"; they have remained in the witch doctor's audience, ignoring the poet's subtle invitation to go backstage.

Beneath and beyond this dazzling exterior display lies Hayden's exploration of this character's psyche. The witch doctor smiles behind the mask as he deludes his followers, but the doctor himself is a study in self-deception. Not coincidentally, Hayden begins and ends the characterization in terms of self-worship. The poem's opening sentence depicts the witch doctor in narcissistic solitude: "He dines alone surrounded by reflections / of himself." His commanding ability "to enmesh his flock in theopathic tension" has led to self-delusion, as Hayden's concluding lines make abundantly clear:

> he dances, dances, ensorcelled and aloof
> the fervid juba of God as lover, healer,
> conjurer. And of himself as God.

While the witch doctor enacts fantasized sexual, physical, and spiritual roles for his followers, he unwittingly dances in fulfillment of his own unconscious needs of similar kind. As a god of his own making, this androgynous figure deceives his "worshipers" to facilitate his own deception. Ironically, he really *is* "as one" with his flock even as he pretends, but in a sense perceived only by the reader.

With characteristic modal versatility Hayden creates another baroque identity with narrative technique and plot circumstance almost the opposite of those used in "Witch Doctor." Rather than a clever, aloof victimizer who deceives with garbled "no-words," "Incense of the Lucky Virgin" features a solitary victim whose disjointed monologue serves as the narrative medium.[34] Using this technique, the poet produces "participatory drama" in the best sense of true dramatic monologues. Without design, the deranged woman unravels her story, implies its frightening consequence, and unconsciously reveals the terrible psychological toll extracted throughout. Once engaged in discerning what she is saying, the reader cannot escape the drama or its thematic implications.

Deserted and destitute, the woman apparently has turned first to cultural superstition and then to religious mythology, both to no avail. Neither conjure ("Incense of the Lucky Virgin, / High John the Conqueror") nor conventional prayer ("My candles held no power") will relieve her plight or "get his children fed." Having more or less rationally described these circumstances as past event, the woman slips into a verbal replay of previously spoken words of instruction to her children. The reader, as yet unaware of the outcome, anticipates some positive action to resolve her dilemma; rather like those children dressed in their Sunday best, the reader tends toward "naïve" hope for an end to the misery. It comes in the indirect yet abrupt revelation of the final stanza, as the persona calmly reports,

> Garland was too quick for me
> (he didn't yell once as he ran);
> Cleola, Willie Mae
> won't be hungry any more,
>   oh they'll never cry and hunger any more.

This understated resolution of dramatic plot, coupled with the speaker's unnerved placidity in reliving the murders of her own children, completes the psychological profile of this modern variation on the Medea theme. Her implicit pathology also "completes" the poem; Hayden leaves open to speculation her status as socio-cultural victim or culprit, the archetypal Medea myth syndrome, and a whole range of possible moral implications. As with some other examples of modern drama, this poetic "mini-drama" is no less powerful for being open-ended.

If the unlucky non-virgin of "Incense" exemplifies Hayden's concern for an "outsider" destroyed by circumstances beyond her ken, his portrayal of "Aunt Jemima of the Ocean Waves" illustrates his admiration for the excluded loners of the world who *can* cope.[35] Interestingly, his initial attitude toward this particular character type (based on a woman he saw working in a Coney Island sideshow) was anything but positive. "Jemima" derives from a four-stanza section of a poem called "from the Coney Island Suite" published in Hayden's *Figure of Time*.[36] Ironically, in view of her later development, Hayden designates the character in that poem "The Unique Original Jemima," but she is merely a name in a brief list of racial stereotypes and physical freaks. Hayden's original speaker protests the "perverted logic" which makes confederates of those in such categories; however, "weary of this stale American joke," he disdains further consideration of the circumstance.

By the time of his "mature" treatment of this theme, Hayden has found more empathy for resilient endurance and great admiration for the endurers. His own life experience no doubt brought about this change in outlook; certainly in "Aunt Jemima of the Ocean Waves" he joins ranks with those same confederates he had avoided in an earlier phase of his poetic development and personal growth. As for the "new" Aunt Jemima, she is the prototype "survivor." Hayden presents her character and story through a dialogue between his narrator and Jemima, but she has all the lines, as their conversation soon gives way to her monologue of reminiscence. The detail of that autobiographical synopsis reveals the strength and subtlety of Hayden's portrait; Jemima's special traits suggest the basis for the poet's admiration of her as a unique "type." Her notable qualities include a wry awareness of her ironic situation, and a complete lack of either self-pity for her past trouble or self-importance for having endured. It is she who calls herself "fake mammy to God's mistakes," but it is Hayden who supplants this image of her with his own vision of her as

> "The Sable Venus" naked on
> a baroque Cellini shell — voluptuous
> imago floating in the wake
> of slave-ships on fantastic seas.

This romanticized view of Aunt Jemima symbolically subsumes her real person, her present "mask" and situation, and even this specific creation. Hayden here and elsewhere depicts human nature as an inclusive image of innate drama, that special quality "beneath the surface" of the ordinary as well as the bizarre.

Because of this insight Hayden can imbue the most mundane of characters with extraordinary qualities. "The Rag Man" is a good case in point.[37] In this brief sketch of a common rag picker, the poet uses the device of psychological projection to offset conventional notions and lend mystery to the persona. The most noticeable aspect of the rag man, as he is viewed walking "the winter streets," is his apparently total independence of the world around him. From the observer-speaker's vantage, this ill-clad, impoverished figure seems impervious to both inclement weather and human contact: "He strides on in his rags and word- / less disdain as though wrapped in fur." This sort of prideful self-sufficiency can be unsettling to one accustomed to regarding such indigents as helpless victims needful of sympathy if not understanding. The rag man's resistance to such "conventional wisdom" initially summarizes his mysterious nature, which prompts the speaker's contemplation.

What little the speaker does know about the past of this "noted stranger" only compounds the mystery; as "the story goes," the rag man long ago "rejected all / that we risk chills and fever and cold / hearts to keep." Hayden's formulation here indicates the speaker's increasing discomfort, and hints at its cause. Ironically, the rag man, who deals in "material" literally, has prompted in the speaker some second thoughts about those materialistic values for which society too often sacrifices its body and soul ("we risk chills and fever and cold / hearts"). Confronted by his own doubts and guilt in the projected personification of the rag man, the speaker resists recognition: "Who is he really, the Rag Man?" In addition to the intrigue provoked by this emphatic inquiry, Hayden also suggests the character's special symbolic identity by consistently capitalizing "Rag Man" through the poem.

Who is he, really? Well, this character allows each reader to be an enlightened King Lear for a moment because the rag man is Hayden's modern version of Lear's "unaccommodated man." As such he represents our unconscious guilt about our materialistic values, the "rags" we covet and collect. Along with Hayden's speaker, we would "like to get shut of the sight of" this mundane figure who makes us face ourselves. Hayden thus translates a common character and an ordinary encounter into an inquiry of almost metaphysical dimension, inviting if not compelling a vicarious sharing of the poem's subtle social and moral implications.

Hayden's affinity for solitary fictional characters with mysterious backgrounds no doubt grew out of the puzzling and troublesome sources in his own life. He frequently addressed the themes of identity and alienation because he literally lived those realities. As he lived them, he also found guarded ways of expressing them. He liked to refer to the general method as "psychic distancing"; the resulting poems partake of the objectifying elements of symbolism and allegory, highlighted by a central persona created to disguise yet reveal Hayden's deepest personal concerns. Naturally, these works provide the most direct (if oblique) path to the poet himself.[38]

One of his earlier works in autobiographical revelation was triggered by a news story about a lost retarded girl who could not identify herself or her origins. Hayden responded emotionally at first, and poetically later, after he had achieved the psychic distance required to convert his experience into the art of "'Mystery Boy' Looks for Kin in Nashville."[39] Paraphrasing the newspaper caption to fit his circumstance and provide a title, Hayden surrealistically reproduces the nightmare of divided loyalties among him and that agonizing abundance of parental figures. They are the mystery boy's "puzzle faces" who alternately "promise him treats" or "hiss and spit at him." Hayden introduces the saving grace of his wife's companionship in the second stanza, figuring Erma Hayden as the mystery boy's "black doll," his "hidden bride." It is she who helps him deal with a past which haunts yet eludes him. Paradoxically, those elders who unknowingly divided Hayden's self are also the only sources of his lost identity. As these ghostly figures "call to him now and then," he can never find them, never hear "the name he never can he never can repeat." Although the poet leaves the mystery boy's dilemma unresolved, he implies the achievement of a sense of present (if not past) "belonging" from his wife's sympathetic understanding. Consistent with the allegorical premise, "his dollbaby wife" provides a sense of security similar to that a lost child might find in a familiar doll. She comforts him as one would a child who has awakened from a recurring bad dream:

> Don't cry, his dollbaby wife implores;
> I know where they are, don't cry.
> We'll go and find them, we'll go
> and ask them for your name again.

Although Hayden found frequent solace in Mrs. Hayden's empathetic support, he also experienced valleys of near despair in his sporadic struggles with emotional, spiritual, and artistic doubt. With the resiliency of an "Aunt Jemima," he endured and later objectified such experience in some of his finest work. Poems like "The Diver" subtly incorporate the personal allegory, but they also transcend personal revelation in their symbolic specificity and universal implication. "The Diver" in particular hosts a multitude of "legitimate," viable readings.[40]

In its most literal sense, as its column-like shape on the printed page suggests, the poem simply recounts the descent and ascent of deepsea exploration, enlivened by vivid description, and dramatically complicated by the speaker's bout with nitrogen narcosis, or "rapture of the deep." On another level, the diver is Hayden enduring the throes of creative impotence, "bottoming out," as it were. One can also see the poem as possibly a veiled delineation of a momentary flirtation with suicide in the diver's desire to get beyond, to "find those hidden / ones, to fling aside / the mask and . . . have / done with self and / every dinning / vain complexity." Given such a reading, those "hidden ones" could be the same "puzzle faces" who called to Hayden in "Mystery Boy."

As an interior monologue, "The Diver" also lends itself to a psychological interpretation of the speaker's psyche. One need not identify Hayden as the diver to sense that persona's desire to abandon the restrictive yet protective bonds of social and moral convention. In that Freudian sense, the poem dramatizes the ongoing contest between the id and the superego. The diver's urge to "unmask" in disregard of identity, conformity, and concealment suggests the power and danger of this unconscious urge. The speaker's uncertainty about the "why" of his survival ("Reflex of life-wish? / Respirator's brittle / belling?") also implies the ambiguity of human behavior attributable to the superego. Who can really know whether social survival is an instinctive or learned behavior? In his original version of "The Diver," Hayden accurately designated the belling apparatus a "regulator"; yet in his final revision he substitutes the technically incorrect term, "respirator."[41] Apparently he wanted to alter his connotation to indicate that he had accommodated the restrictive mask of "The Diver" by viewing it as a life-sustaining necessity rather than as merely a regulatory inconvenience. Whatever the case, the poet closes the poem in keeping with both his fiction and his allegory. The diver does not surface; he only begins his "measured rise," implying both a careful and an uncertain ascent.

Hayden later in his career takes the measure of a completed ascent in his mythic account of his (or any artist's) life, a personal allegory titled "For a Young Artist."[42] He acknowledges his plot source as the story, "A Very old Man with Enormous Wings," by Gabriel García Márquez, but the real story is his own life as an artist.[43] The message of that story, as implied in its title, is "For a Young Artist" aspiring to a life-long commitment to ideals often misunderstood or unappreciated. Hayden as artist is easily identifiable in the poem's persona, "a naked old man / with bloodstained wings," who has fallen to earth "from the August sky" (Hayden was born August 4, 1913; Márquez' "old man" descends in March).

Much of Hayden's allegorical plot concerns public reaction to the mysterious man-creature; in that reaction Hayden characterizes society's ambivalent attitude toward its artists. First, because they cannot communicate with the old man ("neither smiles nor threats, / dumbshow nor lingua franca / were of any use . . . ") or discern his true nature, the people assume his inferiority, put him in the "chickenhouse" with the other winged creatures, and offer him table scraps. In the curiosity stirred by the old man's strangeness, Hayden allegorizes extremes in popular misconceptions of artists in general (and poets in particular?). Those among the "carloads of the curious" willing to pay to see the winged old man seem equally divided: is he "actual angel?" [or] "carney freak?" Some viewers "crossed themselves and prayed his / blessing"; [others] "catcalled and chunked him." Whether regarded "above" society, or a freak of art, the result of this public myopia is the same—an excluded, alien status for the artist.

Through departures from Márquez' story line, Hayden symbolically asserts the proper response of artists to this status, as he both describes his own personal experience and provides instruction to a younger generation of artists. Hayden's narrator makes repeated reference to the old man's nakedness, an element notably absent from the source story, and original with Hayden. The character's refusal to cover himself ("They could not make him hide / his nakedness") symbolizes the artistic commitment Hayden endorses. The artist, in faith to his calling, exposes his soul in his work and his person in his life to the possible misapprehensions of readers, critics, and the general public. Paradoxically, only in this unfettered state can the poet attain the flight of artistic achievement. Unlike the flyer in Márquez' story, who is watched as he flies away, Hayden's old man finally regains the air, unobserved, in the dark of night. His strenuous effort and his achievement go unnoticed:

> He strains, an awk-
> ward patsy, sweating strains
> leaping, falling. Then—
> silken rustling in the air,
> the angle of ascent
> achieved.

The old man's ascent is both the literal high point of the story and the allegorized thematic point of the poem: Hayden thus clarifies the requisite demands for achieving the "angle of ascent," that inner satisfaction which is the ultimate reward of art for artists. Hayden's indirect statement of personal experience neither glamorizes nor demystifies a life devoted to art. The poet graphically represents the hardships in the old man's misunderstood failures and in his unrecognized achievement, but Hayden's use of this mythic story and "baroque" character in itself conveys that mysterious fascination to which so few sacrifice so much.

Hayden explored other personal themes late in his life with similar indirection, but he became more forthcoming in revealing his "inner demons" (as he called them), as in "The Tattooed Man," where he brings together his anxieties about identity, alienation, and artistic sacrifice.[44] Like the winged old man, this persona's "otherness" attracts general attention, yet discourages personal contact. In this instance, however, since the subject is the speaker, the tattooed man can and does share his deepest feelings. In his longing for love, the speaker recognizes that his appearance, his myriad of colorful tattoos, both attracts crowds and repels individuals. He realizes that to those who come to "gawk," he is a "grotesque outsider whose / unnaturalness / assures them they / are natural."

Because Hayden has carefully attributed this alienated condition to the speaker's tattoos in the beginning of the poem, and because he vividly describes some of these figures through the work, one can reasonably assume they have some symbolic significance. Most generally, the tattoos seem to represent the art for which he has suffered; those "masterpieces" needled under his skin are precious to him for both their beauty and their cost: "I clenched my teeth in pain; / all art is pain / suffered and outlived." This conjunction of beauty and pain could also apply more particularly to Hayden's bittersweet perception of self-image, an inner conflict between moralistic repression and the urge of amoral joy. At least the tattooed man describes the detail of his decorations in terms suggestive of the poet's personal demons. Those tattoo patterns repeatedly pair symbolic opposites, juxtaposing conventional Christian myth (and its inherent moral strictures) and the exotic agents of paganism. For example, the speaker locates "Da Vinci's Last Supper— / a masterpiece / in jewel colors / on my breast," in the proximity of "naked Adam / embracing naked Eve," surrounded by "gryphons" and "a gaiety of imps / in cinnabar." Below this configuration, a black widow spider peers from her tattooed web which spans "belly to groin," perhaps suggesting the sexual impulse, also implicit in the "birds-of-paradise / perched on my thighs."

Hayden's tattooed man, like Ray Bradbury's, carries his history etched in his skin. This persona subtly releases the poet's "imps" to gambol for all to see, if not understand. His desire to break through those restraints implanted in his consciousness by birth, upbringing, and cultural influence can find release only in "figurative" dramatization. But the word-pictures suggest what Hayden makes clearer in "Elegies for Paradise Valley." His struggle to escape the sense of unworthiness for having been denied a familial sense of identity was compounded by both the culturally-instilled moralistic guilt he felt as a private person, and the "otherness" he experienced as a public artist. The persona's alienation speaks to all concerned or stricken with this modern plight, but the poet in "The Tattooed Man" is also exorcising his personal demons as he reconciles himself to his unique quandary. The tattooed man initiates his monologue decrying his alien status, wishing "to break through, / to free myself," but he finally accepts both his chronic yearning and his identity: "I cannot / (will not?) change. / It is too late / for any change / but death / I am I."

One can discern a similar acceptance in the balanced perspective of Hayden's confessional voice in "Elegies for Paradise Valley."[45] In this eight-poem recollection of his youth in that ironically-named Detroit slum, Hayden recalls both the horror and joy he associates with a diverse set of inhabitants, including members of his own family. Although these poems eulogize those people, and are thus "elegies" for others, in another sense the entire collection can be regarded as Hayden's retrospective acknowledgment of the two opposed cultural influences on his young life.

The third poem of the set eulogizes "Uncle Henry / (murdered Uncle Crip)" at the scene of his wake. From that seemingly inauspicious beginning, Hayden effectively brings "Crip" back to life and identifies this character with "joy in life," an especially needed commodity in the atmosphere of wasted lives and early death documented in reverie by the poet as the "Elegies" proceed. To begin the sixth poem, he explicitly announces the balance "of death. of loving too:" as he returns to Uncle Crip to illustrate that balance. Speaking directly in a personal confessional voice, Hayden describes his youthful ambivalence toward the cultural dichotomies of death, sin, and life-as-a-vale-of-tears on the one hand, and love and joy on the other. Caught in the middle, Hayden the boy longed for love: "I scrounged for crumbs: / I yearned to touch the choirlady's hair." Of course, such familiarity was as out of place in church as it was taboo in the strict religious morality imposed upon his psyche. Hayden presents the alternative in Uncle Crip: "I wanted Uncle Crip / to kiss me, but he danced / with me instead." He further characterizes Crip as love in the form of outrageous joy, remembering how they danced, "laughing, shaking the gasolier."

In the final "elegy," the poet directly relates Uncle Crip to that inner conflict hinted at earlier. To the righteous "old Christians," Crip is little more than an unrepentant sinner, bound for hell. Even as the boy accepts their view as truth, he also knows that Crip is love and joy. That remembered relative thus embodies and personifies Hayden's dilemma; he could not "sort out" those contraries of joy and sin, love and damnation. He closes the poem in recollection of the resulting guilt: "I knew myself (precocious / in the ways of guilt / and secret pain) / the devil's own rag babydoll." By exteriorizing such memories Hayden artistically objectifies agonies of long standing. In eulogizing Uncle Crip the poet at last releases and celebrates that side of the psychic opposition. Perhaps the ultimate elegy is Hayden's formal, public recognition of the emotional baggage he carried for so long; maybe with "Elegies for Paradise Valley" he was able to store those memories in their proper priority.

Hayden's ultimate, inclusive persona is more "bizarre" than the tattooed man, more "otherworldly" than the winged old man, and yet more expansively public in allegorical articulation of the poet's culminating view of himself, his country, and his countrymen. For "American Journal" he adapts a diary-journal format to create the voice of an extraterrestrial being from another galaxy.[46] This "alien" has been sent to earth to conduct research on America, and to record his observations. Hayden devises a poetic content and structure to make "[American Journal]" read like entries in the persona's logbook. Within this premise the poet provides an "inside look" at an outsider's view, a dramatic monologue in description of American culture, and in revelation of the persona's response to it.

The drama derives from the tension between the persona's supposed scientific objectivity and his increasingly emotional reactions to his observations of, and contact with these "aliens." In this fashion Hayden characterizes America in its best and worst aspects and reveals his own ambivalent feelings about his society. He conveys these feelings by attributing them to his created persona, who can be seen in the journal entries becoming more and more frustrated in his task of cataloging and classifying the amorphous amalgam that is America. Even in the first entry, in spite of its methodical address of purpose and method, the reader can discern portents of emotional crisis. As the alien considers "this baffling / multi people" of "extremes and variegations," and "almost frightening / energy," he considers how he can "best describe these aliens in my / reports." His primary investigative method is assimilation, the ability to take on any identity or human characteristic desired, including "their varied pigmentations," which he "scientifically" judges in his second journal entry to be "the imprecise and strangering / distinctions by which they live   by which they / justify their cruelties to one another."

Successive reports trace a pattern of similar response: beginning with an almost clinical report of fact or inventory, the alien lapses thereafter into a diary-like impression of subjective response to those factual items and concludes the entry by confessing his true feelings. In one typical entry, he first lists geographic features ("oceans deserts mountains . . . "), then acknowledges that these are "vistas reminding me of / home," and ends in confession of his emotional ambivalence toward Americans:

> despite
> the tension i breathe in i am attracted to
> the vigorous americans   disturbing sensuous
> appeal of so many   never to be admitted

Although many entries document contemporary American events and values, in conjunction with the nation's recent past and bicentennial history, the latter portions of the journal again emphasize the alien's fear of failure because he cannot reduce America to scientific precision. By then the reader senses Hayden's point: the reality of America lies in its very resistance to objective analysis. The most literally "alienated" of beings cannot for long resist emotional involvement with this phenomenon of feeling. The speaker's expression of his dilemma constitutes Hayden's view of the people and country he long ago "infiltrated" as a truth-seeking poet:

> america   as much a problem in metaphysics as
> it is a nation earthly entity an iota in our
> galaxy   an organism that changes even as i
> examine it   fact and fantasy never twice the
> same   so many variables

Although no hard evidence of the order of composition supports the notion, one would like to believe that Hayden wrote "American Journal" after "Elegies for Paradise Valley," which in turn followed "The Tattooed Man." "Proof" of that sequence would allow one to generalize that Hayden found personal peace through artistic endeavor at the end of his career, as he reconciled himself to his personal demons, his cultural past, and his national heritage, in that order. In the agonizing process, and through long lean years, he became a "national poet" beyond title or belated acclaim. Robert Hayden may have achieved his "angle of ascent" in 1975, but he did not emerge, "out of the black," (or, better yet, through it) to become America's "laureate" in the Library of Congress.[47] He had, in fact, been writing important poems and evolving from better to best for over forty years. No one noticed until the 1960s, when he had the temerity to stand up for his artistic beliefs, only to be ostracized by one group and ignored by the other. But he never submitted to anything except the demands of his art, as he refused to risk his artistic integrity in return for the fame a wider audience could bring.

It is too late now for the living Robert Hayden to receive the acclaim he deserves, but he is still accessible because he left a legacy of similar souls in the diversity of his poetic portrayals of personages and characters (many who also felt the sting of alienation and neglect). Hayden invested his soul in those characters, so an understanding and appreciation of them as artistic creations can go toward compensating for having "missed" their creator. Although Hayden wanted his work to come first, to take precedence over the facts or myths of his personal life, his soul and craft were entwined. Now we have no choice; the work remains and he is gone. The poet's infusion of his spirit in that work, however, makes choice irrelevant for all who share with Robert Hayden the conviction that a higher truth resides in art.

NOTES

1. Hayden often made this point in his conversations about his poetry. During one interview he said, "I get impatient with people who get too involved with the life and forget the poetry" (Dennis J. Gendron, "Robert Hayden: A View of his Life and Development as a Poet," diss. Univ. of North Carolina 1975, p. 19). Hayden was still expressing similar sentiments when I talked with him in December 1979.

2. "Whereas in Freedom's Name . . . " appeared in Hayden's Hopwood Award-winning manuscript in 1942 and was never reprinted. See also "Crispus Attucks" in Robert Hayden, *Angle of Ascent* (New York: Liveright, 1975), 20.

3. Numerous historical sources reprint the Revere engraving; for example, see Lillian B. Miller et al., *In the Minds and Hearts of the People; Pro-*

logue to the American Revolution (Greenwich, Conn.: New York Graphic Society, 1974), 119.

4. See "Gabriel" in Robert Hayden, *Heart-Shape in the Dust* (Detroit: Falcon Press, 1940), 23–24. For a fictionalized account, consult Arna Bontemps' novel, *Black Thunder* (New York: Macmillan, 1936; rpt. Boston: Beacon, 1968).

5. "The Ballad of Nat Turner" appears in *Angle of Ascent*, 125–27.

6. Robert Hayden, *How I write / 1* (New York: Harcourt Brace Jovanovich, 1972), 183.

7. Ibid., 184.

8. For comparison, see William Styron, *The Confessions of Nat Turner* (New York: Random House, 1967) and John Henrik Clarke, ed., *William Styron's Nat Turner: Ten Black Writers Respond* (Boston: Beacon, 1968).

9. First published in *Phylon* in 1945, "Middle Passage" underwent several revisions before reaching its final form as reprinted in *Angle of Ascent*, pp. 118–23. Cinque was actually a co-leader of the uprising aboard the slave ship *Amistad* off the coast of Cuba in 1839. The fifty-two Blacks killed two of their captors and then forced the two survivors to sail eastward for Africa. The Spaniards thwarted Cinque and his followers by deceptively reversing the ship's course by night. Finally, after meandering up the Atlantic seaboard for over two months, the Spanish slavers were "rescued" and the "slaves" taken into custody off the shores of Long Island. Hayden partially represents the subsequent trial, which concluded with the Supreme Court judgment that the Africans were "self-emancipated" free persons. The thirty-four who survived were returned to Sierra Leone in 1841.

10. For an unusually direct poetic statement of Hayden's ambivalent feelings about God's imminence in the world, see "Electrical Storm" (*Angle of Ascent*, 77–78), a work Hayden called "one of my most personal poems."

11. The John Brown poem was among several collected under the title, "The Black Spear," a grouping Hayden identified in his manuscript as "part of a larger work in progress which has as its theme the Negro people's struggle for liberation and their participation in the anti-slavery movement and Civil War."

12. The poem was initially published in *The Legend of John Brown*, a portfolio of reproductions of Lawrence's paintings; "John Brown" also appeared in the catalogue for the exhibition of the originals in October 1978 before Hayden included it in his manuscript for *American Journal* (New York: Liveright, 1982).

13. "Frederick Douglass" appeared then in the February issue of *Atlantic Monthly*; it has been reprinted since in several Hayden collections, including *Angle of Ascent* (131). The sonnet is perhaps the most widely anthologized of Hayden's poems.

14. *Angle of Ascent*, 128–30.

15. Ibid., 55–58.

16. See Malcolm X, *The Autobiography of Malcolm X*, ed. Alex Haley (New York: Grove, 1964).

17. Hayden's interview comment on this issue is telling: "I believe Malcolm would have come to Baha'i or something like that, close to that" (Gendron, diss., 126).

18. Dennis Gendron also records this typical instance of Hayden's self-perception: "I feel sometimes as though, because I was pulled between two families, two sets of parents, that I have to this hour remained a divided person. One of my problems has been to make myself a whole person, and I had almost to do it; and my faith has helped me . . ." (ibid., 159).

19. See "Names" in *American Journal*, 35.

20. Ibid., 3–4. The salutation, "Dear Obour," is authentic in that Wheatley did in fact write some letters (none from London, though, apparently) to her friend, a Black maid, Obour Tanner (sometimes spelled "Arbour," sometimes "Obur") while Tanner lived in Newport and later in Worchester. For the few surviving examples, see Charles F. Heartman, ed., *Phillis Wheatley: Poems and Letters* (New York, 1915; rpt. Miami, Fla.: Mnemosyne, 1969).

21. *American Journal*, 15.

22. *Angle of Ascent*, 104. See also *How I Write*, 148–49, for Hayden's comments on the poem.

23. *Angle of Ascent*, 6–7.

24. For a prose narrative with a similar subject and theme, see Maya Angelou's essay on Joe Louis in *I Know Why the Caged Bird Sings* (New York: Random House, 1969), ch. 19.

25. *American Journal*, 15. In fact, Hayden was working on a poem about Josephine Baker when he died in February 1980.

26. For the earlier, longer version of "Homage to Paul Robeson," see Michael S. Harper, "Remembering Robert E. Hayden," *The Carleton Miscellany*, 18:3 (Winter 1980), 231–34.

27. *Interviews with Black Writers*, ed. John O'Brien (New York: Liveright, 1973), 112.

28. Gendron, diss., 152–53.

29. *Heart-Shape in the Dust*, 54.

30. *Angle of Ascent*, 110. Although the character is loosely based on the career of Lula Butler Hurst, a gospel singer popular in the Midwest during the 1940s, Hayden needed only the report of her later murder by her lover to stimulate his imagination ("Robert Hayden and Gwendolyn Brooks: A Critical Study," Charles H. Lynch, diss., New York Univ. 1977, 97–98).

31. *Angle of Ascent* 107–109.

32. David Galler, "Three Recent Volumes," *Poetry*, 110 (July 1967), 268.

33. Gendron, diss., 190. A more recent dissertation writer (Charles H. Lynch) finds his own way out of critical controversy; in what he titles "A

Critical Study" of Hayden's work, he simply omits any discussion of "Witch Doctor."

34. *Angle of Ascent*, 106.

35. Ibid., 41–44.

36. *Figure of Time: Poems* (Nashville: Hemphill Press, 1955), 7.

37. *American Journal*, 17.

38. About his purpose and method in such poems, Hayden said, "I'm unwilling, even unable, to reveal myself as directly in my poems as some other poets do. Frequently, I'm writing about myself but speaking through a mask, a persona" (*Interviews with Black Writers*, 16). Although space precludes discussion of those character sketches based on some members of Hayden's family, for a better understanding of his background, consult "Those Winter Sundays," "The Whipping," "The Ballad of Sue Ellen Westerfield," and "The Burly Fading One" in *Angle of Ascent*.

39. *Angle of Ascent*, 38. Speaking of the "mystery boy" persona, Hayden acknowledged, "Oh, that's me, kid, looking for love. The original, the prototype of mystery boy, was a young woman. Yeah, that's definitely autobiographical" (Gendron, diss., 168).

40. *Angle of Ascent*, 75–76. Autobiographical allegory has its inherent risks, however. Some readings could yield unwarranted conclusions such as the thesis that "The Diver" is Hayden's allusive acceptance of the continuing necessity for blacks to "wear the mask," *a la* Paul Dunbar's poem, even if in a slightly more benign form. See Maurice J. O'Sullivan, Jr., "The Mask of Allusion in Robert Hayden's 'The Diver,'" *CLA Journal*, 17, 1 (Sept. 1973), 85–92.

41. See "The Diver" in *Beyond the Blues*, ed. Rosey E. Pool (Kent, England: Hand and Flower Press, 1962), 112–14.

42. *Angle of Ascent*, 8–10.

43. See the story in *Leaf Storm and Other Stories*, tr. Gregory Rabassa (New York: Harper and Row, 1972), 105–12.

44. *American Journal*, 19–21.

45. Ibid., 25–32.

46. Ibid., 57–60. "American Journal" is doubly an "occasional" poem; when the Michigan Chapter asked Hayden to write their 1976 Phi Beta Kappa poem (he had written "The Night-blooming Cereus" in response to a similar request in 1971), he took the occasion to commemorate America's bicentennial year as well. (One hastens to add that this timing *preceded* the subsequent national enthusiasm for films about contact and visitation from outerspace.)

47. As the first Black poet appointed Consultant in Poetry to the Library of Congress, Hayden served during 1976–77 and was again honored by being asked to serve a second term; he returned to the University of Michigan in late summer 1978.

R. Baxter Miller

"Endowing the World and Time": The Life and Work of Dudley Randall

Dudley Randall, poet, librarian, and publisher, is one of the most important Black men of letters in the twentieth century. A child during the Harlem Renaissance, he was himself a leading poet of the subsequent generation of Black writers, and he later became a pioneer of the Black literary movement of the 1960s. His own work, so accomplished technically and profoundly concerned with the history and racial identity of Blacks, benefits from the ideas and literary forms of the Harlem Renaissance as well as from the critical awareness of the earlier Western Renaissance. Although he borrows eruditely from the sources, he culturally transforms them. Through the founding of the Broadside Press and his brilliant editorial work there, he made available to a wide audience the work of fellow poets such as Hayden, Danner, Brooks, and Walker. The variety of such writers indicates that Randall's publishing was in no sense programmatic or intent upon a particular kind of poetry. Indeed, his own skill, so firmly rooted in literary history, is as different in its assumptions from the more formalistic verse of a Brooks or a Danner as it is from the folk and religious poems of Walker. But Randall combines his own poetic credo with that of other poets to create a broad tolerance in what he publishes. In other words, he makes an active commitment to Black literature in general.[1]

Dudley F. Randall was born in Washington, D.C., on January 14, 1914. At the age of four he composed for his own pleasure lyrics for "Maryland, My Maryland," a song played at a band concert in Towson. At age thirteen he won the one dollar first prize for a sonnet submitted to the poet's page of the *Detroit Free Press*. His father, who knew about the Black intellectuals, James Weldon Johnson and W.E.B. Du Bois, took the young Randall to hear them speak at churches. Later the author learned about the post-bellum Black poet Paul Laurence Dunbar as well as the Harlem Renaissance writers. Randall was immediately attracted to the work of Countee Cullen and Jean Toomer, being impressed by Cullen's formal skill and Toomer's use of brilliant imagery. Randall was not yet sixteen years old when he read *Cane*, Toomer's collection of prose sketches. From 1943 to 1946 he served with the United States army in the South Pacific. In 1949 at the age of thirty-five he earned the B.A. degree in English at Wayne State University, and soon afterward (1951) the Master's degree in Library Science at the University of Michigan. After employment with the Ford Motor Company and the United States Post Office for a few months, he became a librarian at Lincoln University (1951–54), Morgan State College [now University] (1954–56), and in the Wayne County Federated Library System (1956–69).[2]

Since that time he has helped to deepen the technical breadth and authenticity of Black poetry. Collaborator and mentor during the Black Arts Movement (1960–75), Randall infused his own ballads with racial history. At Wayne State University he completed all requirements for a master's degree in the humanities, except for writing a thesis, the subject of which was to be a translation of Chopin's music into words. Later, Randall won the Tompkins award in 1962, and after founding Broadside Press in 1965, he won a second Tompkins award in 1966. Boone House, a cultural center founded by Margaret Danner in Detroit, was "home" to Randall from 1962 through 1964. *There* Randall and Danner read their own work each Sunday, and over the years the two of them collected a group of their poems. When Randall edited the Broadside anthology *For Malcolm X*, the prospects for publication encouraged him to bring out the collaborative book as well. Entitled *Poem-Counterpoem* (1966), it became the first major publication of Broadside Press.[3]

Perhaps the first of its kind, the volume contains ten poems, alternately each by Danner and Randall. Replete with social and intellectual history, the verses stress nurture and growth. In "The Ballad of Birmingham" Randall compares racial progress to blossoming. Through octosyllabic couplets and incremental repetition, including a dialogue between a mother and her daughter, he achieves "dramatic reversal," as Aristotle would call it, as well as epiphany. Based on historical incident, the bombing in 1963 of Martin Luther King Jr.'s church by white terrorists, eight quatrains portray one girl's life and death. (Four girls actually died in the bombing.) When the daughter in the poem asks to attend a Civil Rights rally, the loving and fearful mother forbids her to go to the rally. Allowed to go to church instead, the daughter dies anyway. Thus, the mother's concern was to no avail, for an evil world has no sanctuary, either in the street or in the church. After folk singer Jerry Moore read the poem in a newspaper, he set it to music, and Randall granted him permission to publish the lyrics with the tune.

"Memorial Wreath," a Randall lyric of celebration, profits from well-structured analogues. Some imply the processes of resurrection, love, and blossoming. Others draw parallels between ancestry, suffering, and sacrifice; still others liken blues to racial continuity, to the inseparability of pain and beauty, and to the irony of racial experience, including art itself. Finally, when the speaker ultimately addresses his spiritual ancestors, the images come from the American nineteenth century. The more dramatically conceived and frequently anthologized ballad "Booker T. and W.E.B." presents one voice's call and another's response. In alternating stanzas in the poem the two Black leaders (1856–1915; 1868–1963) express opposite views. While Booker T. Washington favors agriculture and domestic service, Du Bois emphasizes the human quest to learn liberally. Despite Washington's focus upon property, Du Bois proposes dignity and justice. Randall, who tries to present each man realistically, favors Du Bois, to whom the narrator gives the last line intentionally. A free verse, "For Margaret Danner / In Establishing Boone House" (December 1962), fuses quest and rebirth into benediction: "May your crocuses rise up through winter snow." And the speaker in "Belle Isle," the last lyric, addresses the poet's calling, "the inner principle . . . endowing / the world and time . . . joy and delight, for ever."

During the first Black Writer's Conference at Fisk University in the 1960s, Randall met Margaret Burroughs, founder and director of the Du Sable Museum of African American History in Chicago. When he called her regarding the anthology *For Malcolm X*,[4] his previous study had prepared him well. He was aware, as most Americans were not, that the father of Russian literature, Aleksander Pushkin, had African origins through a maternal grandfather. Randall, who had learned the Russian language after the Second World War, was able to read the literature in the original, which not only impressed him as much as had the work of Latin and French poets, but had moved him to undertake some translations, notably "Wait for Me" and "My Native Land" by K. M. Siminov.

On his return from Russia and once again at home in Boone House, Randall plunged into cultural activities and met some emerging and important Black writers. He attended art exhibits, jazz sessions, and monthly readings of poetry. Authors read from a new anthology, *Beyond the Blues* (1962), and from a special issue of *Negro History Bulletin* (October 1962). Randall befriended fellow poets Betty Ford, Harold Lawrence, and Naomi Long Madgett as well as Edward Simpkins and James Thompson.[5]

In 1966 Randall met the celebrated poet Gwendolyn Brooks. When a reading club in Detroit invited her to read at Oakland University, he requested that several English teachers meet her at the train station. When he himself finally greeted her after the reading, she was surprised. From book reviews in *Negro Digest*, she had thought him fierce, but he had proved pleasantly mild: "I thought you were terrible, but you're all right." While the two poets took snapshots together, she threw her arms happily around her new friend's shoulders, and, asked later to submit a poem for the new Broadside series, she granted him permission to republish "We Real Cool." He would bring out her pamphlets *Riot* (1969), *Family Pictures* (1971), and *Aloneness* (1971). At first he declined to issue her autobiography, *Report from Part One* (1972), because he believed that Harper and Row could better promote the volume. When Brooks disagreed, he finally conceded the argument, and, upon the publication, Toni Cade Bambara responded enthusiastically on the front page of the *New York Times Book Review*.[6]

With a favorable evaluation of Audre Lorde's first book, *The First Cities* (1966), in *Negro Digest*, Randall followed her progress in *Cables or Rage* (London: Paul Breman, 1970), but, when asked to publish her third book, *From A Land Where Other People Live*, he found himself overbooked. Brooks intervened on Lorde's behalf, however, and he finally relented. The volume, which came out under his imprint in 1973, was nominated for a National Book Award. After the ceremonies in New York he and Lorde went backstage to meet the poet Adrienne Rich. As he paused at the breast-high platform and wondered how to mount it, Lorde gave him a hand. "How's that," she asked, "for a fat old lady?" A representative for Rich's publisher drove the two in a limousine to a cocktail party at the Biltmore Hotel, and Randall wondered secretly when Broadside might afford the luxury of a limousine. Although Lorde had promised to take him on the Staten Island ferry and show him her house in the area, they had celebrated too late; no time would be left during the next morning (*Broadside Memories*, pp. 14-15).

At the writer's conference at Fisk, Randall had strengthened the professional associations that would assure the publication of verses by established poets such as Hayden, Tolson, and Walker in the Broadside series. Securing from Brooks the permission to use the colloquial verse, "We Real Cool," he published the first group — "Poems of the Negro Revolt," a distinguished collection. Although he had the tendency at first to issue famous poems for popular dissemination, a reviewer in *Small Press* suggested that he might serve contemporary writing better by printing previously unpublished verse.

Randall, while at the conference at Fisk, had seen Margaret Burroughs' sketches and heard Margaret Walker rehearse her afternoon reading; as he listened to Walker read about Malcolm X, he observed that most Black poets were writing about Malcolm, and Burroughs proposed that Randall edit a collection on the subject. When Randall invited her to co-edit the volume, she accepted, and David Llorens promised to announce the anthology in *Negro Digest* (later *Black World*). Randall received the first submission a few days later.

For Malcolm X brought Hayden, Walker, and Brooks together with the younger writers LeRoi Jones (Imamu Baraka), Larry Neal, Sonia Sanchez, and Etheridge Knight. Randall, through collaboration with them, learned about the magazines, *Soulbook* and *Black Dialogue*, but problems with the printer delayed publication until June 1967. At Fisk, Randall had seen a slim girl with David Llorens, and, when he returned to Detroit, he received a letter from Nikki Giovanni, who requested a copy of *For Malcolm X* to review in the college publication edited by her. Although *For Malcolm X* did not appear until 1967, after her graduation from Fisk, she reviewed the book for a Cincinnati newspaper (*Broadside Memories*, p. 101). During the book signing by contributors at Margaret Burroughs' museum, he met Haki Madhubuti (then Don L. Lee) and later received a copy of Madhubuti's *Think Black*. The younger poet had himself published 700 copies and sold them all in a week. When he and Randall read for a memorial program at a Chicago high school, Randall advised the new friend, "Now Don, read slowly, and pronounce each word distinctly." Because Madhubuti read first and earned a standing ovation, Randall humorously promised himself to read thereafter "before, not after Don." When visiting Detroit, Madhubuti usually went by Randall's home. Although all business agreements between the two poets were oral, Madhubuti clearly regarded them as binding, for he refused to sign with Random House, and when his second book, *Black Pride* (1968), was completed he asked Randall to provide an introduction. In 1969 Randall brought out Madhubuti's *Don't Cry, Scream* in both paperback and cloth editions, the latter then a first for Broadside, though he himself would later publish a similar edition of *For Malcolm X*.

Over the years Randall won professional warmth from Sonia Sanchez, one of the contributors to *For Malcolm X*. In his poetry class at the University of Detroit she had wondered whether to publish with Third World Press, Madhubuti's firm, or with Broadside, which she finally chose. When Randall had a heart murmur, Sanchez sent him various teas, and, chiding him for smoking, she drove him to bookstores in New York. When he flew to Africa in 1970, she and Nikki Giovanni went to the motel to see him off. For consistent dedication to Black American poetry, Randall won personal and communal loyalty.

Yet Dudley Randall remains a poet in his own right. *Cities Burning* (1968) captures his zeitgist. Here the visionary lyrics and apocalyptic revelations concern urban riot, generational opposition, and Black image-making. "Roses and Revolutions," a prophetic lyric in free verse written in 1948, addresses both the Civil Rights Movement and personal conscience.[7] Two other poems, "The Rite" and "Black Poet, White Critic," clarify in two brief quatrains Randall's theory of art. "The Rite" presents initially a dramatic dialogue and a narrative reflection which in turn give way to the conflict between the old and the young. Symbolically, the drama reenacts the Oedipal struggle between fathers and sons, for to some degree even rebels must cannibalize themselves off the very traditions they seek to overthrow. And insofar as revolutionaries or pseudo-revolutionaries themselves (Randall published many of their works) must emerge at least in part from precisely such tradition, destroying it completely would mean self-effacement. While the writer or any artist wants personal innovation, the younger author internalizes the older one, just as youth seeks to supersede and displace old age. Where such rebellious youth relives the inescapable lessons of the past, for the type of human existence itself never changes, so change itself, even revolution as espoused by militant Blacks in the sixties and early seventies, is necessarily incomplete. In "Black Poet, White Critic" the poet's drama becomes more racially focused as the detached narrator works through humorously to an interrogative punch line. Advising the poet to write "safely," the critic cautions against the subjects of freedom and murder. Moved by "universal themes and timeless symbols," the arbiter proposes a verbal portrait of the "white unicorn," and in quipping back ("a *white* unicorn?"), the narrator underscores the subjectivity of beauty.

Two other poems, "The Idiot" and "The Melting Pot," reveal Randall's technical range. The first, a humorous monologue, blends psychological depth with colloquial tone in order to portray police brutality. The police officer, who has called the speaker a Black "boy," punches him in the face and drags him to the wall. Here the officer searches and cuffs him. Sufficiently angry to chastise the police, the narrator relents because, "I didn't want to hurt his feelings, / and lose the good will / of the good white folks downtown, / who hired him." The irony is complex. The speaker feigns courage, but the rationalization signifies true cowardice. Why did the "good" people downtown hire the demonstrably bad policeman? The speaker's reasoning, ill-suited to an answer, breaks down. Rather than see others in true fashion, the idiot chooses doubly to blind himself. Almost hopelessly naive to white hypocrisy, he misreads direct racism as well. In eight rhymed quatrains "The Melting Pot" (*Cities Burning*, p. 14) illustrates the ironic myth of the American mainstream to the protagonist, Sam. From the presented fable, including the word-play and rhyme, the comic ballad leads to an ultimate epiphany, for thrown out of the American crucible a thousand times, Sam reconfirms, "I don't give a da . . . / Shove your old pot. You can like it or not, / but I'll be just what I am."

Through poems such as "A Different Image," Randall acknowledges the influence of African and Caribbean poets. Schooled well in Négritude, a philosophy espoused by French-speaking Blacks since 1945, he deepens Black experience into universal meaning. In 1968 he brought out James Emanuel's first book of poetry, *The Treehouse and Other Poems* and issued Nikki Giovanni's second book, *Black Judgment*. In the reprinting of Margaret Danner's *Impressions of African Art Forms*, a facsimile of the 1960 original, he redistributed the only known volume devoted entirely to the subject of African aesthetics. During 1969 he published books by poets Jon Eckels, Beatrice Murphy, Nancy Arnez, and Sonia Sanchez, as well as those by Marvin X, Keorapetse Kgositsile, and Stephany. Randall served as instructor of English at the University of Michigan in 1969 and from then until 1974 served as poet in residence at the University of Detroit. For a while at the University of Ghana, he studied African arts. Then he visited Togo and Dohemy. From 1970 through 1976 he completed an appointment to the advisory panel of the Michigan Council for the Arts.

His literary career has prospered; the fourteen poems in *Love You* (1970) achieve more thematic and formal focus than in his previous poetry.[8] With scholarly range, he writes the poem of celebration, the monologue, and the short visionary lyric. Attentive to transitory love-making, as well as to the discrepancy between appearance and reality, he observes well the tension between the tangible and the intangible. Sometimes he uses skillful similes to verbalize a speaker's personal joy; he employs Steinesque wordplay. Through structured dramatic situations, he projects personal advice and consolation for fellows. "The Profile on the Pillow," a well-crafted verse, compares the narrator's trace of the lover's silhouette to the mature poet's commitment to humanity. Set against the race riots of the late sixties, the narrator-lover echoes clearly Brooks's speaker ("The Second Sermon on the Warpland"): "We may be consumed in the holocaust, / but I keep, against the ice and the fire, / the memory of your profile on the pillow." Although love is intangible, the reader recognizes it through the writer's use of tangible light. Retreating from chaotic history, one person asks the other to "step into the circle of my arms," withdrawing from the metaphorical whirlwind and fire, from physical and emotional exhaustion.

For Dudley Randall the early 1970s meant a balanced and personal retreat. Written from the thirties through the sixties, the poems in *More to Remember* (1971) comprise his first comprehensive collection.[9] Although the individual verses are not arranged chronologically, each group represents a particular decade of his work. While times changed, the biting irony and humor developed. *Poem, Counterpoem* (1966) contains only the verses appropriately paired with Danner's, and *Cities Burning* (1968) has only those which reveal a disintegrating era. Then the most indispensible of his volumes, the latter includes the subjects of kindness and cruelty, incredible harvests, diversely classical forms, and natural beauty. Here Randall explores some contradictions in human psychology and in the Black Arts Movement, and, still a thinking poet, in doing so he displays artistic breadth. Adding to the literary strategies from earlier volumes, he draws upon personification, and though despite some occasional and prosaic overstatement he keeps a sharp ear. In deftly manipulating his point of view, Randall writes the lyric or the parable equally well. In "The Line Up," a poem in four quatrains, a police inquiry is written as an extended metaphor. Here one views the worth of various literary periods while the verse employs a double voice. There is, on the one hand, the common speech of accused criminals, including the murderer, the young pimp, and the dirty old man, yet on the other hand, the speaker maintains an ironic detachment; he believes that the investigators ask the wrong questions. Although the police indict many people and record their crimes, the officers themselves hardly understand, nor can they explain the motives.

"Interview," possibly the most sustained and brilliant of the generational poems, portrays an entrepreneur turned philanthropist. As the old man explains his principles to an intruding young reporter, an ambivalence is clearly apparent. The newsman, who has crossed a protective moat and scaled a barbed wire fence, suggests boldly the mirror-image of the philanthropist himself at an earlier age. And in provoking the speaker's own credo, the youngster hears the man repudiate cynicism. The benefactor, self-trained in industry and discipline, avows to "Not snivel . . . prove to those / Who could not take the world just as they found it / And therefore lack the power to change it at all / That one old, greedy and predacious villain / Can do more good . . . than . . . their years of whining and complaining."

"On a Name for Black Americans," a politically angry sermon, stresses self-reliance as well. "The spirit informs the name, / not the name the spirit." While Randall suggests the name Du Bois temperamentally as well as ideally, he pragmatically implies Benjamin Franklin and Booker T. Washington. From childhood he remembers that Blacks worked hard once to have *Negro* capitalized, and he never considered the word derogatory. Although some Blacks have attempted to demean the term by using lower case or by applying it only to the submissive fellows, he still asserts that "what you are is more important than what you are called . . . that if you yourself, by your life and actions, are great . . . something of your greatness will rub off . . . dignify . . . actions affect words . . . In a more limited sense . . . words affect actions" (Randall, "Black Publisher," p. 37).

The distinction between appearance and reality pervades *More to Remember*. "Put Your Muzzle Where Your Mouth Is (or shut up)" addresses sarcastically a theoretical Black revolutionary. Loudly telling others to kill, he has murdered none himself, and the protagonist who shouts "Black Power" in the poem "Informer" similarly deludes the listeners who overlook his whispers to the FBI. "Abu" reveals the contradictions through low burlesque, for the activist who has apparently decided to blow up City Hall advertises in the *New York Times*. Right in front of the FBI infiltrators, he promises to assassinate a white liberal who gave "only" half a million dollars to the NAACP, but, asked to comment later, "Says nothing 'bout that Southern sheriff / killed three black prisoner / 'cept, he admired him / for his sin / cerity." So consumed with self-hatred, Abu is a self-acknowledged coward, for his posture and rhetoric are less dangerous than foolishly deceptive. He criticizes readily some white liberals who pose no obvious threat, but he rationalizes away the need to confront the racist who does so. He is as hypocritical as is the protagonist in "militant Black, Poet," who hangs himself after a white suburbanite downplays the "militant's" bitterness. Finally, the poem "Ancestors" exposes the revolutionary's own elitist tendencies. While such people fantasize about royal heritage, they demean humble origins. In "On Getting a Natural (For Gwendolyn Brooks)," the volume's final poem written in December 1969, Randall's speaker celebrates the humanist. At first too humble to admit her own charisma ("beauty is as beauty does"), Brooks blossoms into racial awareness, and her epiphany rings true.

In *More to Remember* the description concludes with Randall's aesthetic theory. In "The Ascent" he has represented the poet as visionary, and in "The Dilemma (My poems are not sufficiently obscure? To please the critics — Ray Durem)," he has revealed once more the tension in the artist, the modifier of both literary tradition and classical form. Whether from traditionalists or revolutionaries, the artist asserts intellectual independence. The appropriately titled "The Poet" illuminates the type. Sloppily dressed and bearded, the writer reads when he should work. Imagining a poem, he would rather turn a profit and convert to "outlandish religions"; he consorts with Blacks and Jews. Often disturbing the peace, a "foe of the established order," he mingles with revolutionaries. In a satirical ploy the narrator plays temporarily the bigot's part: "When will you [the poet] slough off / This preposterous posture / And behave like a normal / Solid responsible / White Anglo Saxon Protestant." Randall's artist philosophizes more than he lives ("The Trouble with Intellectuals"), but he feels deeply ("Mainly By the Music").

Especially from 1972 through 1974, Randall contributed much to

Black American culture. He participated in a poetry festival, "The Forerunners," codirected by Woodie King at Howard University in 1972.[10] He bolstered indirectly the early success of the Howard University Press, which would issue the proceedings, and in Washington he heard Owen Dodson read from a wheelchair. He listened to Sterling Brown present "Strong Men." A recipient of the Kuumba Liberation Award in 1973, Randall participated in the seminar for socio-literature in the East West Culture Learning Institute at the University of Hawaii. He had established himself, says Addison Gayle, as one "who came to prominence, mainly, after the Renaissance years, who bridged the gap between poets of the twenties and those of the sixties and seventies . . . began the intensive questioning of the impossible dream, the final assault upon illusion that produced the confrontation with reality, the search for paradigms, images, metaphors, and symbols from the varied experiences of a people whose history stretches back beyond the Nile."[11]

Dudley Randall marks well the transition over six decades. His next pamphlet, *After the Killing* (1973), often assumes the style and voice of the younger poets.[12] Although most of the verses included are recent, some are older ones. "To the Mercy Killers" appears with some poems completed during the sixties and seventies. Here Randall experiments with typographical lyrics and sharpens Juvenalian satire. Despite others' inclinations toward modern compression, he avoids the direction of Wallace Stevens and Gwendolyn Brooks as well as the visionary sweep of Walt Whitman and Langston Hughes. Pausing occasionally for sexual deliberations, he lays bare intraracial prejudice and semantic deceptions. "Words Words Words" criticizes Black activists who constantly favor white and light-skinned women. When the expressions belie the deeds, Randall's speakers toy with ambiguities. While one Black says "fag—" means something else, another adds that "mother" does as well. The narrator concludes that "maybe black / doesn't mean black, / [two line space] but white." The double space underscores the pause and insight.

The title poem, a parable, infuses murder with the solemnity of biblical myth. The literary world transmutes the poet's life into fable, for the historical Randall lived through World War II and Viet Nam. As in Robert Hayden's "In the Mourning Time," the speaker distills Black anger into ritual. Supposedly dedicated to ultimate peace, the bloodthirsty man kills other people, whose children in turn kill his own. Another bloodthirsty one, three generations later, repeats the original's words: "And after the killing/there will be [triple or quadruple space] peace." The blank space implies human extinction or an undesired solution. "To The Mercy Killers" translates the ritual more clearly into social portraits of totalitarianism and abortion, though neither subject may be fully intended. One man reclaims sarcastically the glowing life from others, the self-appointed gods who would destroy him. Elsewhere Randall's narrator states aphoristically: "There are degrees of courage. / One man is not afraid to die. / A second is not afraid to kill. / A third is not afraid to me merciful."

With energy and commitment, Randall demonstrates Black self-determination now. Influenced more by modernist techniques, he discusses the love of writing and the joy of publishing. Despite the fun of teaching, he expects his professional and literary career to take new turns. While not tearing up his work, he writes only in the days he has time. He composes the poems in his head and then writes them later — sometimes while lying down or driving along the freeway.

Randall believed that young Black poets should be free from publishers like Random House and Morrow and, despite the emergence of new talents, that older poets should continue to be active. While abandoning sonorousness in his own art, he attempted looser forms and more colloquial diction. Wanting a widely diverse audience, Randall worked for richness and philosophical depth. To achieve freedom and flexibility he declined partnerships as well as incorporations, for he feared that stockholders would demand profits, would lower quality, or would publish prose. While his income from the press went into publishing new poetry volumes, Randall paid royalties to other poets. He confessed, "I am not well qualified to operate in a capitalistic society. I came of age during the Great Depression, and my attitude toward business is one of dislike and suspicion. Writers who send me manuscripts and speak of 'making a buck' turn me off." Although dedicated to ideals, Randall remembered well the pragmatic lessons from the Black Renaissance. When the Depression came in the thirties, white publishers had dropped Blacks who earlier had been popular, so Randall recommended that Afro-Americans "build a stable base in their own communities" (Randall, "Black Publisher," pp. 34-36).

In "Coleman A. Young: Detroit Renaissance" the speaker advocates communal rebirth.[13] Aware of contemporary mechanization, he still acknowledges the value of wisdom. The historical sweep, suggesting both racial and human consciousness, spans 3,000 years. The final lines allude at once to Langston Hughes' *Montage* and Shakespeare's *Tempest*:

> Together we [human community] will build
> a city that will yield
> to all their hopes and dreams so long deferred.
> New faces will appear
> too long neglected here;
> new minds, new means will build a brave new world.

The rhythmically intoned "long" and the repetitive "new" achieve sound inflections, ones rare indeed in more formal Black poetry. Even the words of Shakespeare's Miranda ("brave new world") assume a bluesesque depth and a suspended sharpness in half-stepped musical climbs.

Randall's recent book, *A Litany of Friends* (1981), demonstrates an intellectual depth of themes used and technical mastery of the poetic form.[14] Of the eighty-two poems collected, twenty-four are reprints, and forty-eight are new. Six poems appeared first in *Poem, Counterpoem* (1966), four in *Cities Burning* (1968), one in *Love You* (1970), fourteen in *More To Remember* (1971), and nine in *After the Killing* (1973). Grouped topically, the verses demonstrate Randall's technical skill.

Randall enlarges the humanness of poetry written in English. Sensitive to Robert Hayden's historical allusions, he employs the sea-death imagery of Alfred Lord Tennyson, and he alludes equally well to Thomas Gray's graveyard school or to the blues tradition of Langston Hughes and Sterling Brown. Responsive to both romance and tragedy, Randall achieves the lyrical as well as the dramatically stoic poem. Creating both inner and outer voices, the private persona and the detached narrator, he reveals human consciousness.

In the sustained title poem of forty lines, Randall celebrates other people. Here are family members and fellow artists who helped him through a severe personal depression in the mid-seventies. While metaphors and similes emphasize kinship as well as journey, familial embrace signifies communal ritual. The ceremonial tone leads back through Black America to Africa. Without the mention of last names, the speaker thanks Gwendolyn Brooks for remembering him and sending gifts. He praises the late Hoyt Fuller for respecting him as a man rather than as a hero. In his mind he hears Etheridge Knight tell him to confront the pain and to transcend it. While the speaker thanks Audre Lorde for writing and sending donations, the narrator praises Sonia Sanchez, who phones him and sends herbs. So, friendship inspires personal restoration.

Two other poems, "My Muse" and "Maiden, Open," suggest Randall's erudition. Well-versed in the poetic themes and forms of antiquity as well as in the English Renaissance, he shows the ambivalence of art and eternal love. In the seven stanzas of "My Muse" (October 1, 1980), he blends Greek sources with African sound. While the muse ("Zasha") inspires the poet, his verses come either in tenderness or wrath. The speaker observes classical analogues between the African muse, Catullus' Lesbia, and Shakespeare's dark lady as well as Dante's Beatrice and Poe's Annabel Lee. Restored to her rightful place in human mythology, the African muse appears as, "My Zasha / Who will live for ever in my poems / Who in my poems will be forever beautiful." The blackness is sublime. Through the analogue between the poem and the damsel, "Maiden, Open" places eternalness equally against the enchanted landscape: "who ever tastes the poet's lips / Will never grow old, will never die. . . ."

More political poems such as "A Leader of the People (for Roy Wilkins)," written April 18, 1980, and "A Poet Is Not a Jukebox" distill racial history into literary type. Although Wilkins, an NAACP leader, was still alive then, today the verse marks an appropriate threnody. Dramatized in two voices, the optimistic one written in roman type and the pessimistic one expressed in italics, the poem contrasts Wilkins with the skeptical narrator. And, on a second level, it sets up Wilkins' two selves, one visionary and the other pragmatic. Wilkins acknowledges a commitment to self-respect and independence, but the negative voice assures him that sacrifice earns the enduring hatred of men and women. When Wilkins answers he will risk hatred for love, the counterpart argues that others will rebuke him. Whereas Wilkins agrees to bear scorn and pride for the sake of Blacks, the other responds demonically so. Although Wilkins reaffirms the mission to withstand the enemies and save the people, the pessimist finishes introspectively: "It is not your enemies who will do these things to you, / but your people."

When the emphasis falls less upon betrayal than endurance, "A Poet Is Not a Jukebox" reaffirms an artistic independence. After writing a love poem, the speaker must defend the choice to a militant inquirer. Why, she asks, doesn't he portray the Miami riot? Now self-removed from social upheaval, he has worked lately for the Census and listened to music. In ignoring television, he has avoided the news as well. As a statement about artistic freedom, the poem leads through totalitarianism to a complexly human statement. The writer must achieve personal and emotional range, for out of love and the commitment to happiness and joy, he "writes about what he feels, what agitates his heart. . . ."

Apparently Randall edits in the same manner. While some scholars would view Randall today primarily as a publisher, others think of him as a man of letters. While he fails to shape his talent into polished rhythms and compressed images, he writes keenly in the ballad and sonnet forms, and in prophetic verse, he experiments in the parable and fable. Although attracted to the poetry of antiquity, including classical conventions, he also gives his energetic support to modern originality. While enabling him to perceive the love often overlooked in the poetry and life of Sonia Sanchez, his sensitive ear also helps him to appreciate the epic tone and Christian analogue in verses by Etheridge Knight, Sonia's former husband. Whether or not Dudley Randall is a great poet in his own right, Black American literary art has benefited from his great talent and love for fifty years.

NOTES

1. Charles H. Rowell, "In Conversation with Dudley Randall," *Obsidian*, 2:1 (1976), 32–44; Dudley Randall, "Black Publisher, Black Writer: An Answer," *Black World*, 24, v (1975), 32–37; Richard Barksdale and Keneth Kinnamon, "Part VI: Since 1945," in *Black Writers of America: A Comprehensive Anthology* (New York: Macmillan, 1972), 808–809.

2. *Who's Who Among Black Americans* (Northbrook: Ann Wolk Krouse, 1980), 657.

3. Margaret Danner and Dudley Randall, *Poem, Counterpoem* (Detroit: Broadside Press, 1966).

4. Margaret G. Burroughs and Dudley Randall, eds., *For Malcolm X* (Detroit: Broadside Press, 1967).

5. Dudley Randall, "Margaret Danner and Boone House," *Broadside Memories: Poets I Have Known* (Detroit: Broadside Press, 1975), 36.

6. Randall, "Audre Lorde," *Broadside Memories*, 14–15.

7. Dudley Randall, *Cities Burning* (Detroit: Broadside Press, 1968).

8. Dudley Randall, *Love You* (London: Paul Breman, 1970).

9. Dudley Randall, *More to Remember* (Chicago: Third World Press, 1971).

10. Woodie King, Jr., ed., *The Forerunners: Black Poets in America* (Washington, D.C.: Howard Univ. Press, 1981).

11. Addison Gayle, Jr., "Introduction," *The Forerunners*, ed. King, xxiii–xxiv.

12. Dudley Randall, *After the Killing* (Chicago: Third World Press, 1973).

13. Dudley Randall, "Coleman A. Young: Detroit Renaissance" in *Broadside Memories*, 20.

14. Dudley Randall, *A Litany of Friends* (Detroit: Lotus Press, 1981).

[*Editor's Note*: In separate letters of 30 September and 22 October 1985, Naomi Long Madgett, founding editor of Lotus Press, responded to a draft of this essay. She maintains that the development of the Detroit group of poets should be credited to Rosey E. Pool. Through her television program, "Black and Unknown Bards," and her personal associations, Pool organized a "loosely knit group" of Black poets and performers. For years Oliver La-Grone and Madgett had given readings in Detroit, and as far as they knew they were the "only serious black poets around." Madgett says that "I had never heard of Dudley Randall but met him during this time. A group of us met regularly at Boone House, which Margaret Danner did indeed inhabit, having talked the minister whose church owned the structure into letting her stay there, in spite of its lack of heat, proper plumbing, etc. We met more often on Friday nights, and we took turns reading from our own work. Dudley no more 'lived' there than the rest of us, except for Margaret, and he was no more a leader than of the rest of us."]

Erlene Stetson

Dialectic Voices in the Poetry of
Margaret Esse Danner

Margaret Esse Danner, an ironist and imagist, informs her poetry with an extensive knowledge of the world both personal and public. Her concerns include art, music, history, dance, folklore, and religion. A word conjuror and artisan, she provides her reader with well-crafted "word sketches" that are impressionistic and expressionistic. Her poetry, the result of a dialectic between voices of her past, present, and future, reveals her role and relation to a tradition of Western poetics; her artistic invention of poetry as a visual impression combines graphic social criticism and visual creation, that which is both didactic and mimetic, into an exciting synthesis of a new aesthetic; her verse makes her reader a viewer of art (synesthetic imagery) as well. Architectural imagery, referential setting, and rhetoric are a few of the strategies used by Danner.

Here I shall trace the evolution of her literary voice from the subjects which inform her growth and development. This discussion opens with the personal images and codes that distinguish her voice. Finally, it will close with a consideration of her formal logic and her literary theory.

The literary awakening known as the Harlem Renaissance had been a decade nearer when Danner was born in 1910. Today two cities, Detroit and Chicago, claim her; she was actually born in Chicago, where she has lived and worked, though she has recently lived in Memphis, Tennessee.[1] Danner's early poetic career began with "The Violin," a prize-winning poem written when she was an eighth grader. In 1945, she was a winner in the Midwestern Writers Conference at Northwestern University. In 1952, she won a John Jay Fellowship. In 1956, she served as assistant editor of *Poetry: A Magazine of Verse*. In the 1960s she established cultural art centers in both Chicago and Detroit.

Her poetry has appeared in several anthologies and numerous periodicals.[2] She has associated, at least as regards ideas, with Karl Shapiro and Paul Engle of *Poetry Magazine* and later with Langston Hughes and Robert Hayden. Her family, her religion (Bahai), her Black life, including her travels to Europe and Africa, have all been poetic sources. Her extensive friendships with her art mentor Edna Moten and the poets Dudley Randall and Haki Madhubuti, as well as with Margaret Burroughs, Margaret Walker, Nikki Giovanni, and Gwendolyn Brooks, often find a reference in her poetry.

Danner writes poetry on a diversity of subjects. She treats the life of an African worm with as much sensitivity as her own artistic development. It is, however, Africa that exerts a coercive pull on her imagination. Relying heavily on the images of sight and sound, she demands the involvement of her audience. Based on the premise that poetry must be accessible, and Archibald MacLeish's dictum that a poem should not mean but be, her verse entertains as well as teaches. Almost all her poems advance from the personal and specific to the general and universal. Her critical sense is informed by knowledge, craft, and training, all necessary for revealing the creative imagination.

Overall, her poetic technique signifies method and strategies which place the reader in one of two broad groups. While one includes those who appreciate poetry, the other accounts for the skeptics. Mediating between the extremes, she reconciles both groups. With considerable adroitness and skill in "Like Breaths," she finely demystifies the creative process. She makes poetry a simple art that unifies:

> Individuals ideas — like breaths —
> are waiting to be drawn
> from unlimited supply.[3]

Her patterned repetition of words (sigh, sighing, hiss, hissing) contribute to the sound of the poem, and from the semantic point of view, the repetition deepens the meaning of the poem by operating in association.

Danner's poetry, a perceptual process, makes intelligible what would otherwise be complex. On the surface "The Down of a Thistle" seems to be deceptively simple, and simple things are a part of Danner's art. But, far more subtle, the image merges and metonymically embodies a deeper truth of a historic race (p. 12):

But there are many thistles who
having had no royal passage
were seized and thrown into "holds"
slumping over humps of humiliation, degradation,
making spines of their many lumps
in order to protect their crowns.

Danner universalizes the trope into the symbolic situation where
hardship overshadows beauty:

And the stonier the path
the thornier the thistle
until now nearly everyone is so busy
avoiding the thorns
that few get near enough
to enjoy the down.[4]

Written mostly in free verse and end rhyme, Danner's poetry uti-
lizes allusion, irony, symbol, and concrete imagery that place her in
a poetic tradition. The reader discovers the imagism of Ezra Pound,
Amy Lowell, Helene Johnson, and Hilda Doolittle, especially the im-
pressionism of the Harlem Renaissance, and notably, Helene John-
son, whose verse "Trees at night"[5] closely resembles her own. Yet
Danner's poetry does more than invoke Countee Cullen's fantasy
Africa of "spicy grove and cinnamon tree"[6] or Gwendolyn Bennett's
nostalgic and dreamy Africa of darkness, romance, mystery, and
imagination.[7]

She approximates Langston Hughes in simplicity of subject and
theme and Robert Hayden in style and tone. Her poetry bridges the
gap between a didactic nineteenth-century Black poetry of racial pro-
test and racial pride and the Harlem Renaissance (1920s) poetry, distin-
guished by rhetorical exaltation of a romanticized blackness. Cultural
assumption, historical background, the poet's own background and
literary tradition provide contexts for Danner's poetic imagination.

Danner's Africa, the predominant subject of her poems, is both
real and symbolic, for she writes of a living, vibrant, and dynamic
African culture. She explores private and public myths to arrive at
an authenticated African past. Indeed the poet's books, all published
in the sixties, surpass the limitations of the New Black Poetry Move-
ment in its sheer ability to create a context that includes temporal
and historical backgrounds avoiding the lure of the didactic posture.

She chooses poetry over polemics, proving she is a better poet than politician. She chooses self-exploration as a means to rediscover an authentic Black past. A poet activist, Danner set up numerous Black poetry workshops during the sixties. The reader sees in her a Black woman writing in creative tension against the mainstream society that would deny her African roots, and a Black woman poet writing in the self-conscious discipline of the strategic possibilities of her life and art. The reader sees Danner the artist without losing sight of Danner the Black woman. The critical appreciation that she engenders in her reader is one that includes and then transcends the exigencies of tribe, nation, language, gender, and socio-political condition. Her real world merges effortlessly with her imagined one. Although Countee Cullen in "Heritage" invokes an imaginary Africa with the rhetorical question of racial dearth ("What is Africa to Me?"),[8] out of a sense of frustration and incompleteness, Danner does not do so. She writes poems like "Her Blood, Drifting Through Me, Sings," on the contrary, where the Black (not "Dark") continent represents only one fount from which she drinks; she visits, explores, studies, understands the "cultural cathedral." She appreciates it as both an inspiration (for creativity) and a condition of her life:

> Africa: I turn to meet
> this vast land of bitter-sweet.
> Africa: whose creviced walls
> cradle myriad waterfalls.
> Africa: where black men stride
> toward freedom's ever inching tide.[9]

Meaning and mood in this poem as in her other poems on Africa, are characterized by vivid and sensuous details of the empirical world (Africa) balanced by the literary one that she creates with pen and ink.

Out of her quest to know and to penetrate the mystery of existence, Danner's poetry chronicles her own artistic growth and development. Her poem "The Convert" dates her "rebirth." Here history, autobiography, and artistic eternality, the last which resists imposing time, become a metonym for aesthetic structure:

> When in nineteenth-thirty-seven, Etta Moten, sweet-
> heart
> of our Art Study group, kept her promise, as if
> clocked,
> to honor my house at our first annual tea. . . .[10]

Here she marks the first sign of the African art initially rejected.

Ironically, while the poet's knowledge allows her to dismiss the African nude, the same knowledge, upon reflection, makes it accessible. Her self-reflective strategy allows for rearrangement and readjustment which make for intelligible perception. Alienated by the ethnocentricity of a Western education, the poet, through mental searching, reorientates and reclarifies her perception of art. Her ten stanza poem, "Etta Moten's Attic," details her inchoate gropings in poetry via the metonymy of sculpture, the metonymy of weaving:

> It was as if Gauguin
> had upset a huge paintpot
> of his incomparable tangerine,
>
>   .   .   .   .
>
> masques and carvings and paintings not seen
>
>   .   .   .   .
>
> spun geometrically in Ndebele rug
> flung over an ebony chair.[11]

Moving from the unfamiliar to the familiar, the speaker takes the reader from ignorance or innocence to enlightened experience. The conclusion of "The Convert" concerns a new birth, a new discovery:

> . . . I became a hurricane
> of elation, a convert, undaunted who wanted to
>   flaunt
> her discovery, flourish her fair-figured-find.

As does the rhyming couplet of "Etta Moten's Attic" ("quickening and charming till we felt the bloom / of veldt and jungle flow through the room"), the poet emphasizes process rather than the achievement.

Danner feigns ignorance in a Socratic way to undercut the reader's cultural snobbery. Since ignorance is the starting point, the strategy for coping is re-education, which emerges not from erudition in the accomplished arts ("Art clubs like leaves in autumn, fall / scrabble against concrete and scatter"[12]) but from the poet's curiosity and versatility.

Richly allusive and written in free verse, her poems evoke a central controlling image, i.e., both a palm wine jug or a bronze carved head, exist as visual images and embody symbolic meanings as well. Her use of verbs shows skillful percision and proficiency. She becomes both an artist of temporal song and an artisan of sculptured form. Elements of architecture in her poems are gold, bronze, sandalwood,

ebony, and ivory. Her colors are "muted sheens" of tangerine, in-
digo, ivory, and brown. [13]

Typologically, she is reminiscent of the mythical Daedalus who pre-
cedes her. The artful artificer, from which the word "art" comes to
mean craft (artisan) according to legend, invented the then unknown
art, the technology of flight. To escape the labyrinth in which he is
imprisoned, the first artist cum craftsman, makes himself wings with
feather and wax. He fits these to his own body and to that of his
son Icarus. Metaphorically imprisoned between Africa and Amer-
ica, Danner's narrator seeks to liberate herself from the conflict be-
tween aesthetic and cultural judgments:

> But I find myself still framing word sketches
> of how much these blazing forms ascending
>   the centuries
> in their muted sheens, matter to me. [14]

In Danner's poetry, Africa is both the subject and object of a new
aesthetic appreciation, enabling her to soar above the quotidian ba-
nalities of indifference, hostility, and ignorance. Discovering the
complementary harmonies of an African nude, the poet gains the
spatial and internal perspective through which the properities crystal-
ize for discernment and study ("a radiance, gleaming"). [15] The poet's
epiphany comes in contemplating an African schema, a pattern for
relevant truth. Dispelled of ignorance, the reader not only "sees" the
objects of African art but appreciates African culture through an
intimate awareness:

> This two-toned sandalwood stick was of pencil height.
>   It had been
> tapered at one end until it resembled a pencil's
>   reversed steeple
> And carved into a stork with a lifted leg; who began to
>   preen
> and probe at an affinity for a form, vaporing between
>   my mind and my memory. [16]

Rightfully associated here with invention, civilization, and art, the
Ovidian mode best explains Danner's poetry. [17] The form illustrates
the complementary dimensions of written language through a tem-
poral dimension one first experiences and then recognizes as a whole.

Finally, the qualities of the spatial perspective and structure avail themselves to serious study.

"The Convert" illustrates the author's methodology that plays upon confusion and struggle to reveal the African nude's symmetry and structure. The process of fusing these distinct (at least initially) phases (struggle and appreciation; ignorance and knowledge; error and truth) demonstrates the dynamic and dialectic principle. Meaning appears through mental searching and re-arrangement.

From a philogicial standpoint, a glossing of the world "art" may well illuminate Danner's literary theory. In the IndoEuropean etymology, "Art" means "to fit," "to join";[18] it originally denotes fitting things together but has come to connote skill, dexterity, artifice or cunning, craftsmanship, or strategy. With elaborate cunning, Daedalus excels in assembling parts. Danner particularly brings together disparate cultures (Africa and America) and disciplines (the plastic arts and poetry). Her forms emphasize not so much the final result of the process but the process itself. Art becomes an act rather than an object; knowledge rather than information, the practical result.

Her poetic technique involves logic. She employs a Socratic form to advance her point. As did Socrates and Plato, she reduces the many, the conflicting, and contradictory into systemically organized concepts. Her poems "The Elevator Man Adheres to Form" and "The Slave and The Iron Lace" demonstrate intellectual investigation. Here the poet sets up a dialectial tension through which opposing viewpoints subtly reveal ironic truth.

"The Elevator Man Adheres to Form" consists of six stanzas. The first and sixth one have a formal end-rhyme scheme (a-b-a-c); the second, third, fourth, and fifth ones are three-line sections with interconnected rhyme schemes at the end. The poem concerns two divergent groups within Black culture, and the poet desires a union between the two.

The first group is symbolized by the "Rococo" elevator man who elevates ("wings") himself and impresses the reader through his ritual:

> I am reminded, by the tan man who wings
> . . . . His ways
> are undulating waves that shepherd and swing
> us cupid like from floor to floor.

Moved by her artful wit, the poet turns to the less erudite men mired in misery:

> . . . I vision other tan and deeper
>   much than tan
> early Baroque-like men who (seeing themselves
>   still
> strutlessly groping, winding down subterranean
> grottoes of injustice, down dark spirals) feel
> with such torturous, smoked-stone grey intensity
> that they exhale a hurricane of gargoyles. . . .[19]

Desiring a union between "the tan man" and the "tan and deeper much than tan" men, the speaker wishes that" . . . this elevator artisan would fill his flourishing form / with warmth for them and turn his lettered zeal / toward lifting them above their crippling storm."

Alienation, accommodation, and ambivalence inform both profiles. Their warring images describe well Danner's two groups of readers, those clothed in erudition and those hopelessly ignorant of any other than their suffering dark selves. The metaphors of contrast are color ("tan and deeper much than tan") and movement ("undulating waves," "crippling storms," and "subterranean grottoes"). They mark real as well as symbolic actions ("strutlessly groping" and "greetings, God-speedings. . . ").

Ironically, both men waste themselves either through the empty performance of ritual or in the allowance of themselves to destruction through misery and self-pity. The speaker sees salvation in transcending their type of minds, for their actions imply another kind of thematic unity. Evocations of the baroque and the rococo externalize verbally their grotesqueness into architectonic form.

Appropriately concerning a mason, the monologue, "The Slave and The Iron Lace" contains four stanzas, the third and fourth of which are repetitive. Here the aesthetic form teaches us, infusing creativity with irony and insight. At first, the straight narrative belongs to the artisan:

> The craving of Samuel Rouse for clearance to create
> was surely as hot as the iron that buffeted him.
> His passion for freedom so strong that it molded
> the smouldering fashions he laced.[21]

Freedom has a double meaning: it is both physical and artistic. "Iron" has a historic ring, referring equally to the slave status as well as the property of the art. There is irony because only in his "passion for freedom" could Rouse discover "the mold" for the "smouldering fashions he laced." His "passion for freedom" not only shapes his art but helps him to discover the "mold" to "create" the "delicate Rose and Lyre," the complex "Grape" and "Classic vein into an iron bench." The mature speaker questions:

> How could he wind the Grape Vine,
> chain the trunk of a pine with a Round the Tree,
>   Settee
> Mold a Floating Flower tray,
> create all this in such exquisite, fairyland taste,
>   that he'd
> be freed and his skill would still resound
> one hundred years after?

Not only does Danner recreate and retrieve significant "lost" Black history, but she shows how a viable art can be created out of both an artistic and a social imperative even as she shows that creativity occurs to many. While the one may occur through race or condition, the last two may expand rather than limit art. Her metaphors are as effective as light, airy, delicate lace. Like heavy and smouldering iron, the contradictions inform the terms slave and artisan, free and enslaved. And the slave who discovers his freedom in creating becomes mentally free despite physical servitude. The situational irony translates into a Hegelian premise.

But the question of the undramatized listener, the young Black militant, converts personal reflection into universal empathy:

> And I wonder if I, with this thick asbestos
>   glove
> of an attitude could lace, and bend this ton
> of lead-chained spleen surrounding me?
> Could I manifest and sustain it into a new free-
> form screen
> of not necessarily love, but (at the very least
>   for all
> concerned) GRACE.

Here the images structure Danner's artistic credo.

From the classical dichotomy between lyric and rhetoric, to the poetics of the twentieth century, her poetry merges to clarify the dialectic voices which shape it. But her complex and eclectic art resists easy categorization and reduction. Her "word sketches" both move through and, like all good art, transcend genetic histories. The double perspective marks her voice. A final (and probably intended) irony is that even aesthetic freedom betrays possibly the deeper need for the real kind of liberty.

NOTES

1. Danner was Poet in Residence at Le Moyen-Owen from 1970 to 1975.
2. Her poems appear variously in magazines and journals that include *Chicago Review, Negro Digest, Black World, Negro History Bulletin, Accent, Poetry, Voices, Chicago Magazine,* and *Quicksilver.* Her published works are *Impressions of African Art Forms in the Poetry of Margaret Danner* (Broadside Press, 1960); *To Flower: Poems,* N.P. Hemphill Press, c. 1963; and *Poem, Counterpoem* (with Dudley Randall, Detroit: Broadside Press, 1966); *The Down of a Thistle: Selected Poems, Prose Poems and Songs by Margaret Esse Danner* (Waukesha, Wis.: Country Beautiful, 1966; (Millbrook, N.Y. Poetic Press and Print, at Kriya Press, 1968). She has edited two anthologies of students' verse: *Brass Horse* (1968) and *Regroup* (1969). The original edition of *Impressions of African Art Forms* was published in 1960 by Contemporary Studies of the Miles Poetry Association of Wayne State University. *Margaret Danner and Dudley Randall Read Poem Counter Poem* (Recording, 1966; Margaret Esse Danner, *Not Light, Nor Bright, Nor Feathery* Detroit: Broadside Press, 1968)
3. Margaret Esse Danner, *The Down of a Thistle: Selected Poems, Prose Poems and Songs by Margaret Esse Danner.* (Waukesha, Wis.: Country Beautiful, 1966). 11.
4. Page 12. See "The Negro National Anthem: "Stony the Road We Trod." This poem, "Lift Every Voice and Sing" by James Weldon Johnson, can be found in most anthologies of Black poetry.
5. Helene Johnson has no published book, though her poetry is variously anthologized. See *Black Sister,* ed. Erlene Stetson (Bloomington: Indiana Univ. Press, 1981).
6. Countee Cullen's poem "Heritage" appeared in his first published work, *Color* (New York: Harper & Brothers, 1925).
7. See *Black Sister,* For Bennett's poem "Heritage": "I want to hear the chanting Around a heathen fire / of a strange black race."
8. Cullen, *Color.*
9. *Impressions of African Art Forms*; also see *Iron Lace* (Millbrook, N.Y.: Kriya Press, 1968); *The Down of a Thistle: Selected Poems, Prose Poems, and Songs by Margaret Esse Danner.* Waukesha, Wis.: Country Beautiful, 1966.
10. *Impressions of African Art Forms.*
11. This poem appears in *The Down of a Thistle.*

12. "The Convert," *Impressions of African Art Forms.*

13. "Amsac," ibid.

14. See note 12.

15. Ibid.

16. "The Two-Toned Stork of a Hairpin, This Comb" in *The Down of a Thistle* and *Iron Lace.*

17. Ovid, *Metamorphoses*, trans. Frank Justus Miller (London: Heinemann, 1960). I am indebted to my Joycean colleague Fritz Senn for his readiness to converse on the subject.

18. See J. Skeat, *An Etymological Dictionary of the English Language* (Oxford: Oxford Univ. Press, 1909).

19. See *Iron Lace* and *The Down of a Thistle*, 68.

20. *The Down of a Thistle*, 103.

21. *Iron Lace.*

[*Editor's Note*: See also June M. Aldridge, "Langston Hughes and Margaret Danner," *The Langston Hughes Review*, 3 (Fall 1984): 7–9; idem., "Margaret Esse Danner," in *Dictionary of Literary Biography*, ed. Trudier Harris and Thadious M. Davis, 41 (Detroit: Gale, 1985), 84–89.]

Richard K. Barksdale

Margaret Walker:
Folk Orature and Historical Prophecy

Like Robert Hayden and Melvin Tolson, Margaret Walker has written her poetry in the shadow of the academy. Both of her advanced degrees from the University of Iowa — the master's degree in 1940 and the Ph.D. in 1966 — were granted because of her achievements in creative writing. Her first volume of poems, *For My People* (1942), won the Yale Series of Younger Poets Award and helped her to gain the master's degree; her prize-winning novel, *Jubilee*, fulfilled the central requirement for the doctorate. But Margaret Walker's poetry is quite different from that written by Hayden or Tolson. Many of Hayden's poems are full of intellectual subtleties and elusive symbols that often baffle and bewilder the reader. *Harlem Gallery*, by Tolson, is often intellectually complex and obscure in meaning. Margaret Walker's's poetry, on the other hand, is clear and lucid throughout, with sharply etched images and symbols presented in well-formed ballads and sonnets. It is now clear in retrospect that Hayden and Tolson were influenced by the academic poets of the 1930s and 1940s — Ciardi, Tate, Lowell, Wilbur, Auden, Dickey. Their poetry has an academic gloss, suggesting richly endowed libraries in the sophisticated suburbs of learning. Only rarely do they seem sensitized to problems and dilemmas confounding an unintellectualized, urbanized, and racially pluralistic America, a concern which dominates Margaret Walker's poetry.

Although Walker, too, spent all of her days in academia, she was never as a writer held captive by it. An analysis of her poetry reveals that in subject, tone, and esthetic texture, it is remarkably free of intellectual pretense and stylized posturing. One finds instead the roots of the Black experience in language simple, passionate, and direct. If one asks how Margaret Walker as a writer remained in the academy but not of it, the answer appears in the circumstances governing her family life and background.

Margaret Walker was the daughter of a preacher man, and not just an ordinary one. Her father, Sigismond Walker, was a native of Jamaica who, in 1908, four years before Claude McKay's arrival in 1912, came to America to study at Tuskegee. Unlike the poet McKay, however, Sigismond Walker persevered academically, gained a degree at Atlanta's Gammon Theological Institute and then joined that small band of educated Black methodist ministers who ventured forth to preach the Word in the pre-World War I South. So Margaret Walker grew up in a household ruled by the power of the word, for undoubtedly few have a greater gift for articulate word power than an educated Jamaican trained to preach the doctrine of salvation in the Black South. Indeed, personal survival in the Walker household demanded articulateness. The poet admits that in a home filled with song and singing inspired by her musician mother, she struggled successfully to survive without the gift of song; but survival without the mastery of words and language was impossible. So by the age of twelve, Margaret Walker was writing poetry and sharpening her communication skills; and, when, at the age of seventeen, she transferred from New Orleans' Gilbert Academy to Northwestern, she took her well-honed verbal skills with her. As noted in *How I Wrote Jubilee*, she quickly discovered at Northwestern that she did not know how to convert the rich orature of her talking, word-filled New Orleans household into a novel, but she was fully convinced that she had carried the power of the word with her to Evanston.

Not only was there a preaching father in the Walker household, but there was a talking maternal grandmother — a grandmother full of tales of "befo' dah wah" and "duin da time afta da wah." So there were stories to be listened to and placed in the vault of memory. And there was also New Orleans with its rich background of folk mythology, its music, its red beans and rice and jambalaya, and its assortment of racial experiences to be remembered and recalled through the power of the word.

So Margaret Walker as a poet and as a writer was not dependent on the academy for her subject matter, for her style, for her authorial posture. Indeed, the rhetorical power of the poem, "For My People" — the verbal arpeggios, the cascading adjectives, the rhythmic repetitions — has its roots in the "preacher-man" rhetoric of the Black South.

Similarly, Vyry's eloquent prayer in *Jubilee* came from the Blacks' past and from the deep folk memories of a trouble-driven people.

The poet would also be the first to admit that her "down-home" grounding in the principles of the Judeo-Christian religion, Black-style, protected her against the frivolous intellectualism of the academy. She had no need to join movements, to bow to trends, and identify with esoteric cults. Her religion also stood her in good stead when, in 1935, she graduated from Northwestern and joined other writers in Chicago's rather radical WPA Writer's project—writers such as Nelson Algren, Richard Wright, Studs Terkel, Willard Motley, James Farrell, and Jack Conroy. In 1935, Chicago lay by the shore of Lake Michigan like a beached whale, panting its way through the Depression, and the world and Chicago were ripe for social and political revolution. Racism, gangsterism, corruption, and political radicalism were everywhere. But Margaret Walker kept her home-grown faith through it all, calling not for violent revolution but for "a new earth" that would "hold all the people, all the faces, all the adams and eves."

The poet's career started out with a bang. In 1942, when, at twenty-seven, she published her first volume of poems—*For My People*—she became one of the youngest Black writers ever to have published a volume of poetry in this century. Langston Hughes had published "The Negro Speaks of Rivers" at the age of nineteen, but his first volume of poems was not published until 1926 when he was twenty-four.[1] Moreover, when her volume won a poetry prize in 1942, Margaret Walker became the first Black woman in American literary history to be so honored in a prestigious national competition. But these achievements are not what is notable or significant about *For My People*. The title poem is itself a singular and unique literary achievement. First, it is magnificently wrought oral poetry. It must be read aloud; and, in reading it aloud, one must be able to breathe and pause, pause and breathe preacher-style. One must be able to sense the ebb and flow of the intonations. One must be able to hear the words sing, when the poet spins off parallel clusters like

> . . . the gone years and the now years and the maybe years,
> washing ironing cooking scrubbing sewing mending hoeing
> plowing digging planting pruning patching dragging along.

This is the kind of verbal music found in a well-delivered down-home folk sermon, and, as such, the poem achieves what James Weldon Johnson attempted to do in *God's Trombones*: fuse the written word with the spoken word. In this sense the reader is imaginatively set free to explore what Shelley called the beautiful "unheard melody" of a genuine poetic experience. The passage is also significant in its emphasis on repetitive "work" words describing the age-old labors of Black people. The activities are as old as slavery—slavery in the "big house" or slavery in the fields. Adding "ing" to these monosyllabic work-verbs suggests the dreary monotony of Black labor in slave times and in free times. Without the "ing," they remain command words—enforcing words, backed up by a white enforcing power structure. And behind the command has always lurked the whip or the gun or the overseer or the Captain or the boss or Mr. Charlie or Miss Ann. Indeed, Black laborers, long held captive by Western capitalism, were forced to work without zeal or zest—just "Dragging along." Somehow they remained outside the system of profit and gain; no profits accrued to them for their labor; thus, they dragged along, "never gaining never reaping never knowing and never understanding." In just these few lines, Margaret Walker performs a premier poetic function: she presents a succinct historical summary of how the Black man slipped into an economic and social quagmire when, first as a slave and then as a quasi-free man, he was forced to cope with the monster of European capitalistic enterprise.

Not only does *For My People* have word power, but it is a poem filled with subtle juxtapositions of thought and idea. When the scene shifts from the rural South to the urban North—to "thronging 47th Street in Chicago and Lenox Avenue in New York"—the poet describes her people as "lost disinherited dispossessed and happy people." At another point, they are depicted as "walking blindly spreading joy." This Donnesque yoking of opposites linking happiness with dispossession and blind purposelessness with joy reveals the depth of Margaret Walker's understanding of the complexities of the Black experience. In fact, the poet here is writing about the source of the Black peoples' blues, for out of their troubled past and turbulent present came the Black peoples' song—a music and a song that guarantee that happiness and joy will somehow always be found lurking behind the squalor of the ghetto or behind the misery of the quarters or in some sharecropper's windowless cabin in the flood-drenched lowlands. For whenever there is trouble, a Bessie Smith or a Ma Rainey or a Bill Broonzy or a B.B. King or someone with the gift of song will step forward to sing it away. In fact, the song gets better when one is real lowdown and disinherited and even suicidal:

Goin' down to the railroad
Put my head on de track
Goin' down to the railroad
Put my head on de track
When No. 3 come rollin in
Gonna pull ma big head back.

So, although misery and woe are ever-present in the Black community, suicides remained low. If things got too bad, there is always tomorrow; so one sang, "Hurry sundown, see what tomorrow bring / May bring rain / May bring any ol' thing." As the poet indicates, joy and misery are always juxtaposed in the Black experience.

Margaret Walker also states that Blacks die too soon, the victims of "consumption and anemia and lynching." Each word in this triad of death has its own history in the Black experience. Consumption (or the more clinical but less poetical word tuberculosis) became a famous word in the white experience when it became "the white death" that ravaged the industrial nations during and after the Industrial Revolution. No capitalistic society was spared; and, since it was highly contagious, it quickly spread from white mill hands and miners to all levels of the Western capitalistic society. Famous poets and artists — Keats, Dunbar, Dumas' "Camille," Rosetti's "Elizabeth Siddal" — died of consumption. Indeed for some the dying cough became a very romantic way to depart this troubled earth. For those, however, who lived on the fringes of the capitalistic nations — Blacks, Indians, Eskimos, Polynesians — consumption was devastatingly genocidal. Unprotected by medical strategies of any kind, the dark-skinned minorities died like butterflies in a mid-winter blizzard. On the other hand, anemia was different. It was and is the Blacks' disease of the blood, the result of their centuries-long battle against malaria in their African homeland. In building up an immunity against one dread disease, Black people ironically inherited a capacity for incurring another dread disease. So anemia had deep roots in the Black peoples' past — like their love of yams or their love for the chanting tribal drums.

On the other hand, lynching, the final word in the poet's triad of death, was different from the other two causes. Lynching had no deep roots in the history of the Black person's past: it was not transported from Africa, but rather was a uniquely "American" practice that blended well with a brutally exploitative economic system. Essentially, the lynching of Black males was the Southern white male's response to the Black man's inferred sexual superiority; for, usually, the lynched Black was castrated before he was burned or hanged, even if he had not been accused of a sexual crime. In this way the guilt-stricken white South expressed its fear of the Black man's imputed sexual vigor. To date, Margaret Walker has not published a poem elaborating on this particular topic of racial sexual rivalry in the South, but in a recent interview, she comments on the matter in an interesting fashion.[2] In her opinion "Sexual warfare" exists because "there's a mirror image of racism in the South." The poet explains:

> What white men see in black men, black men see in white men. . . . The worst thing in the world [for the white man] was a black man with a white woman. . . . The worst thing in the world [for a black man] was a black woman with a white man.

The bloody tide of lynchings that swept the South from the years following the Civil War into the mid-twentieth century indicates that Blacks, powerless and politically helpless, lost the battle for sexual equality. And the poet is right. Only Blacks die of lynching; history does not record a single instance of a white man's being lynched because he raped a Black woman.

Two additional comments about "For My People" should be made. First, according to the poet's own recollection, she needed just fifteen minutes to compose it on her typewriter.[3] The poem is thus comparable in composition time to Langston Hughes' "The Negro Speaks of Rivers," which Hughes states that he wrote while crossing the Mississippi River enroute on a long train ride to visit his father in Toluca, Mexico.[4] Second, the poem is comparable to McKay's sonnet, "If We Must Die," in its breadth of universal appeal. It struck a chord of vibrant response in pre-World-War II America, and it became the rallying cry twenty-five years later during the strife-torn 1960s. If the test of a great poem is the universality of statement, then "For My People" is a great poem.

Although one cannot say that the rest of the poems in Margaret Walker's initial volume meets the same criteria for high poetic quality, they reflect the young poet's sense of "word power" and her sharp awareness of the importance of Black orature. The poems in Part II contain a series of Black folk portraits — Poppa Chicken, Kissee Lee, Yallah Hammuh. In many of these, one can trace the influence of Langston Hughes' 1927 volume of poems, *Fine Clothes to the Jew*, which contained many verses portraying Black folk and celebrating the Black urban life style. Indeed both Poppa Chicken and Teacher remind one of Hughes' "Sweet Papa Vester" in that poet's "Sylvester's Dying Bed." All three are sweet men — men who pimp for a living and generally walk on the shady side of the street. There are differences, however, between the Hughes portrait and those by Margaret Walker. Hughes' version is comically objective. Nowhere does the author obtrude an opinion in the brief story line, and everything, as in any good comic routine, is grossly exaggerated. As he lies dying, "Sweet Papa Vester" is surrounded by "all the wimmens in town" — "a hundred pretty mamas" — Blacks and "brown-skins" all moaning and crying. On the other hand, both "Poppa Chicken" and "Teacher," written in a swinging ballad rhyme and meter, lack the broad comic touch one sees in the Hughes poem. In fact, the protagonist is a "bad dude" and not to be taken lightly:

> Poppa Chicken toted guns
> Poppa wore a knife.
> One night Poppa shot a guy
> Threat'ning Poppa's life.[5]

Teacher similarly has no comic stature. In fact, it is the poet's opinion that

> Women sent him to his doom.
> Women set the trap.
> Teacher was a bad, bold man
> Lawd, but such a sap!   (p. 44)

Three other poems in Part II of *For My People*, "Kissee Lee," "Long John and Sweetie Pie," and "Yallah Hummuh" reflect a Hughesian influence. Although all three are written in a swinging ballad rhyme and meter that Hughes never used in his Black folk portraits, they all reveal a finely controlled and well-disciplined narrative technique. There is just enough compression of incident and repetitive emphasis to provoke and sustain the reader's interest. And all of the characters — Long John, Sweetie Pie, Kissee Lee, and Yalluh Hamma — come from the "low-down" social stratum where, Hughes believed, Black men and women lived in accordance with a life style that was to be treasured simply because it was distinctively Black. Theirs is an environment filled with heroic violence, flashing knives, Saturday night liquor fights, and the magnificent turbulence of a blues-filled week-end of pleasure and joy. For instance, after Margaret Walker's Kissee Lee "learned to stab and run" and after "She got herself a little gun,"

> . . . from that time that gal was mean,
> Meanest mama you ever seen.
> She could hold her likker and hold her man
> And she went thoo life jus' ra'sin san'. (p. 38)

To the Kissee Lees of the world death comes soon and

> . . . she died with her boots on
>   switching blades
> On Talledega Mountain in the likker raids. (p. 39)

The ballad "Long John Nelson and Sweetie Pie" presents another story which has been repeated many times in Black folklore—the story of a very stressful romantic relationship that ends in disappointment, separation, grief, and death. There is the inevitable triangle involving Long John, who is ever a lover but never a laborer; Sweetie Pie, who cooks real good and eats far too well; and a "yellow girl," who has "coal black hair" and "took Long John clean away / From Sweetie Pie one awful day." The brief story ends when Sweetie Pie, her lover gone, wastes away and dies. To historians and literary scholars, it is a story of small, almost mean, insignificance; but to a Black folk poet interested in the rich orature of her people, this little story opened another window on the world of the Black experience.

Part II of Margaret Walker's first volume of poetry also includes poems about "Bad Ol' Stagolee" and "Big John Henry," Black mythic folk heroes whose stories have been told and sung for generations. Since both men really lived and died, the poet in recounting their stories dips into authentic Black folk history. John Henry, the steel-driving man who would not let "a steam drill beat him down," was employed in the Big Bend Tunnel in West Virginia on the C&O Line and lost his life in a tunnel accident in 1872. Similarly, Stagolee, born in Georgia shortly after the Civil War, became a Memphis gambler who was widely known for his big stetson hat, his .44, and his ever handy deck of cards. When a fellow gambler named Billy Lyons objected to the way Stagolee shuffled the cards and, in a fit of anger, knocked off Stagolee's stetson and spit on it, Stack promptly shot him dead with his .44. In her poetic version of the John Henry and Stagolee stories, Margaret Walker does not restrict herself to the known historical facts. She shifts through the accretion of myth and incident and, in swinging couplets, tells how "Bad Man Stagolee" shot, not Billy Lyons, but "a big policeman on 'leventh street" and how John Henry was a "sho-nuff man / Whut lived one time in the delta lan'" in the Mississippi cotton country. Both men are larger than life heroes. For his murder of a white policeman, Stagolee is never caught, and no one knows how he eventually died; all that is known is

> Bad-man Stagolee ain't no more
> But his ghost still walks up
>   and down the shore
> Of Old Man River round New Orleans
> With her gumbo, rice and good
>   red beans!   (p. 35)

On the other hand, the poet tells us how her John Henry died — "a ten-poun hammer done ki-ilt John Henry." But the manner of his dying is not nearly as important as his symbolic fame as the preeminently gifted Black laboring man. He stands for all Black men who, amid great adversity, farmed and plowed, dug and hammered, lifted and strained throughout the South to build railroads, load steamboats, and tote bricks in "the bilin' sun." But Margaret Walker embellishes her John Henry with even more heroic attributes. He consorts with witches who

> taught him how to cunjer,
> And cyo the colic and ride the
>   thunder.   (p. 49)

He can whistle like a whippoorwill and talk to the "long lean houn." In other words, in addition to being the symbolic Black laboring giant, he has supernatural gifts that lift him far above humankind's mortal sphere.

One other poem in this section of *For My People* merits some comment. "Molly Means" is a well-crafted poetical description of "a hag and a witch; Chile of the devil, the dark, and sitch."

> Imp at three and wench at 'leben
> She counted her husbands to the number seben.
>   O Molly, Molly, Molly Means
> There goes the ghost of Molly Means.   (p. 33)

Apparently, Molly is a sorceress, in some way related to the New Orleans conjure women that Margaret Walker knew so much about. It is also apparent that the setting for Molly's witchery is rural, for farmers fear that she will blight their crops for

> Sometimes at night through the shadowy trees
> She rides along on a winter breeze.   (p. 34)

What is interesting about the poem is that it was written in the mid-1930s, shortly after the period known as the Harlem Renaissance had drawn to a Depression-induced end, but in no way does the poem reflect, in theme or in style, the poetry of that period. Like the title poem of the award-winning volume, "Molly Means" speaks with a new voice in Black American poetry. It is not a poem of racial or romantic protest, nor does it ring with social or political rhetoric. Rather it is a poem that probes the imaginative vistas where witches and elfins dwell — a poem that demands "a willing suspension of disbelief." And, as indicated above, "Molly Means," in its balladic simplicity, is a far cry from the carefully cerebrated poetical statements coming from the poets of the academy during the mid-1930s.

In the 1940s and 1950s, Margaret Walker published a few occasional poems (later gathered for publication in a Broadside Press volume, *October Journey*, in 1973); but, in addition to attending to her responsibilities as wife, mother, and college professor, she devoted most of her "literary" time to researching historical and biographical data for her fictional magnum opus, *Jubilee*. When this novel was published in 1966, the South was already ablaze with the Black protest against segregation and the century-long denial of the Black people's civil rights. The events of that period — the bombings, the deaths, the marches, the big-city riots — stimulated the most exciting outburst of Black poetry since the Harlem Renaissance. These poets, with some significant exceptions, were young urban revolutionaries who were conscientiously abrasive in their racial rhetoric. Not only did they insist that wrongs be righted, but they assumed a para-military posture and demanded that the guilty be punished by fire, by bullets, or by the sheer violence of their poetic rhetoric. Inevitably, the seething racial turbulence of the times provoked a poetical response from Margaret Walker. Because of her experience, background, and training — her familial gift of word power, her intensive apprenticeship in Chicago's literary workshop in the 1930s, and her mastery of Black orature—her *Prophets For a New Day* (Broadside Press, 1970) stands out as the premier poetic statement of the death-riddled decade of the 1960s. The poems of this small volume reflect the full range of the Black protest during the time— the sit-ins, the jailings, the snarling dogs, the 1963 March on Washington, the lynching of the three Civil Rights workers in Mississippi. All of the poems in the volume touch the sensitive nerve of racial memory and bring back, in sharply etched detail, the trauma and tension and triumphs of that period. "Birmingham" and "For Andy Goodman, Michael Schwerner and James Chaney" stand out as carefully wrought poetical reactions to a city and to an event that filled the world with horror and foreboding.

Both of these poems are unusual simply because painful emotions are not recollected in tranquillity but in moods carefully textured by the delicate filigree of the poet's imagery. For instance, in "Birmingham" the first part of the poem is filled with the persona's nostalgic memories of the beauty of the Birmingham countryside as the twilight settles over the red hills. In this section of the poem, the reader senses the God-wrought beauty that enfolds the city—a city filled with the evil that man has wrought.

> With the last whippoorwill call of evening
> Settling over mountains
> Dusk dropping down shoulders of red hills
> . . . .
> Cardinal flashing through thickets—
> Memories of my fancy-ridden life
> Come home again.[1]

Part II of the poem is concerned with death and the images of dying. The principal persona of the poem has returned to a city engulfed by it—a city "where a whistling ghost" makes "a threnody / Out of a naked wind."

> I died today.
> In a new and cruel way.
> I came to breakfast in my night-dying clothes
> Ate and talked and nobody knew
> They had buried me yesterday.   (p. 14)

In Part III the persona longs to return to her "coffin bed of soft warm clay," far from the North's "bitter cold." For Birmingham and the

South, drenched in the blood of countless Black martyrs, are good places in which to die and be buried.

The lines dedicated to the memory of Goodman, Schwerner, and Chaney, the young Civil Rights martyrs murdered by klansmen in Mississippi's Neshoba County, are also rich in imagery and symbol. There is no rhetoric of confrontation, but there is a very successful effort to filter through the nuances of memory and find the three young men again. One remembers, first, three faces — one "sensitive as the mimosa leaf," one "intense as the stalking cougar," and the third as "impassive as the face of rivers." And then one remembers that the summer of their death cannot last forever and that soon fall will come and the three young men will metamorphose into three leaves, cut adrift from life and mixing helter-skelter with nature's superb fall potpourri of wind, water, and sunlight.

Then the poet turns directly to the lives of the three young men to probe how a century of concern can be reduced to a quintessential moment in the "hourglass of destiny." Cut off prematurely, they will never know the "immortality of daisies and wheat," "the simple beauty of a humming bird," or "the dignity of a sequoia" — never know the full meaning of winter's renunciation or spring's resurrection. And who murdered the sensitive Goodman, the intense Schwerner, the impassive Chaney? The poet exercises her poetic license to castigate with a forceful alliterative phrase those who killed and entombed the three young men:

> The brutish and the brazen
> without brain
> without blessing
> without beauty. . . .

Before closing the poem, Margaret Walker once again examines the startling contradiction between the South's languorous natural beauty and the ugliness of Black lynched bodies floating in muddy rivers or buried in soggy graves shaded by fragrant magnolias and stately live oaks. The South is full of parodoxes, but the juxtaposition of floral beauty and bloody violence is the most puzzling. And nowhere is this more obvious than in Mississippi.

In the final section of *Prophets for a New Day* Margaret Walker turns to history and prophecy, linking today's Black leaders, old and young, to the biblical prophets. The volume's title poem begins with "the Word," but the final lines of the title poem throb with the poet's indignation and outrage about the unfettered power of the beast of racial hatred that roams the land.

> His horns and his hands and his lips are gory with
>   our blood.
> He is War and Famine and Pestilence
> He is Death and Destruction and Trouble
> And he walks in our houses at noonday
> And devours our defenders at midnight.
> He is the demon who drives us with whips of fear
> And in his cowardice
> He cries out against liberty
> He cries out against humanity.   (p. 23)

The poems that end the volume of poetry present in brief portraits the "Prophets for a New Day" — Benjamin Mays (Jeremiah), Whitney Young (Isaiah), Martin Luther King, Jr. (Amos), Julian Bond (Joel), and Medgar Evers (Michah). These poems with their strong religious content prove that Margaret Walker has come full circle from the biblical source for social history back to biblical parable. She begins and closes with the Word. In the "breaking dawn of a blinding sun," she offers a promise that "the lamp of truth" will be lighted in the temple of hope and that, soon one morning, "the winds of freedom" will begin "to blow / While the Word descends on the waiting World below."

Langston Hughes, in his review of Gwendolyn Brooks' *Street in Bronzeville*, stated that all good poets are more far sighted and perceptive in discerning social problems and ills than politicians.[6] Of Margaret Walker he would have noted her great gift for prophecy and the marvelous word power that enabled her to burrow deeply into the rich orature of her people.

NOTES

1. Paul Laurence Dunbar published his first volume of poetry, *Oak and Ivy*, in 1892, a few months after his twenty-first birthday.

2. John Griffith Jones, interview with Margaret Walker, in *Mississippi Writers Talking* (Univ: Univ. of Mississippi Press, 1983), II, 140–41.

3. Ibid., 133.

4. Langston Hughes, *The Big Sea: An Autobiography* (New York: Knopf, 1940; rpt. Hill and Wang, 1963), 33–34.

5. Margaret Walker, *For My People* (rpt. New York: Arno Press and the New York Times, 1968), 36. The volume appeared originally in the Yale University Series for Younger Poets (1942).

6. *Opportunity* (Fall 1945), 222.

R. Baxter Miller

The "Intricate Design" of Margaret Walker: Literary and Biblical Re-Creation in Southern History

Margaret Walker learned about Moses and Aaron from the Black American culture into which she was born. As the daughter of a religious scholar, she came of age in the Depression of the thirties, and her career, like those of Margaret Danner, Dudley Randall, and Gwendolyn Brooks, has spanned three or four decades. Much of her important work, like theirs, has been neglected, coming as it does between the Harlem Renaissance of the 1920s and the Black Arts Movement of the 1960s. Most indices to literature, Black American and American, list only one article on Margaret Walker from 1971 through 1981.[1]

Walker knew the important figures of an older generation, including James Weldon Johnson, Langston Hughes, and Countee Cullen. She heard Marian Anderson and Roland Hayes sing, and she numbered among her acquaintances Zora Neale Hurston, George Washington Carver, and W.E.B. Du Bois. What does the richness of the culture give her? She finds the solemn nobility of religious utterance, the appreciation for the heroic spirit of Black folk, and the deep respect for craft.[2] Once she heard from the late Richard Wright that talent does not suffice for literary fame. She took his words to heart and survived to write about his life, his self-hatred, and his paradoxical love for white women.[3] She knew, too, Willard Motley, Fenton Johnson, and Arna Bontemps. Walker's lifetime represents continuity. From a youthful researcher for Wright, she matured into an inspirational teacher at Jackson State University, where she preserved the spirit of her forerunners, the intellect and the flowing phrase, but she still belongs most with the Black poets whose careers span the last forty years. Her strengths are not the same as theirs. Mar-

This essay is reprinted from *Tennessee Studies in Literature*, 26 (1982), 157–72.

garet Danner's poetry has a quiet lyricism of peace, a deeply con-
trolled introspection. No one else shows her delicacy of alliteration
and her carefully framed patterns. Dudley Randall's success comes
from the ballad, whose alternating lines of short and longer rhythms
communicate the racial turmoil of the sixties. He profits from a touch-
ing and light innocence as well as a plea and longing for the child's
inquiring voice. Purity for him, too, marks an eternal type.

In *For My People* Walker develops this and other paradigms in
three sections, the first two divisions with ten poems each and the
last segment with six. The reader experiences initially the tension
and potential of the Black South; then the folk tale of both tragic
possibility and comic relief involving the curiosity, trickery, and de-
ceit of men and women alike; finally, the significance of physical and
spiritual love in reclaiming the Southern land. Walker writes careful
antinomies into the visionary poem, the folk secular, and the Shake-
spearian and Petrarchan sonnets. She opposes quest to denial, his-
torical circumstances to imaginative will, and earthly suffering to
heavenly bliss. Her poetry purges the Southern ground of animosity
and injustice that separate Black misery from Southern song. Her
themes are time, infinite human potential, racial equality, vision,
blindness, love, and escape, as well as worldly death, drunkenness,
gambling, rottenness, and freedom. She pictures the motifs within
the frames of toughness and abuse, of fright and gothic terror. Wild
arrogance for her speakers often underlies heroism, which is often
more imagined than real.

The myth of human immortality expressed in oral tale and in lit-
erary artifact transcends death. The imagination evokes atemporal
memory, asserts the humanistic self against the fatalistic past, and
illustrates, through physical love, the promise of both personal
and racial reunification. The achievement is syntactic. Parallelism,
elevated rhetoric, simile, and figure of speech abound, but more
deeply the serenity of nature creates solemnity. Walker depicts sun,
splashing brook, pond, duck, frog, and stream, as well as flock,
seed, wood, bark, cotton field, and cane. Still, the knife and gun
threaten the pastoral world as, by African conjure, the moral "we"
attempts to reconcile the two. As both the participant and observer,
Walker creates an ironic distance between history and eternity. The
Southern experience in the first section and the reclamation in the
second part frame the humanity of folk personae Stagolee, John
Henry, Kissee Lee, Yallah Hammer, and Gus. The book becomes a

literary artifact, a "clean house" that imaginatively restructures the Southland.

But if Dudley Randall has written "The Ballad of Birmingham" and Gwendolyn Brooks "The Children of the Poor," Walker succeeds with the visionary poem.[4] She does not portray the gray-haired old women who nod and sing out of despair and hope on Sunday morning, but she captures the depths of their suffering. She recreates their belief that someday Black Americans will triumph over fire hoses and biting dogs, once the brutal signs of white oppression in the South. The prophecy contributes to Walker's rhythmical balance and vision, but she controls the emotions. How does one change brutality into social equality? Through sitting down at a lunch counter in the sixties, Black students illustrated some divinity and confronted death, just as Christ faced His cross. Walker deepens the portraits by using biblical typology, by discovering historical antitypes, and by creating an apocalyptic fusion.[5] Through the suffering in the Old and New Testaments, the title poem of *For My People* expresses Black American victory over deprivation and hatred. The ten stanzas celebrate the endurance of tribulations such as dark murders in Virginia and Mississippi as well as Jim Crowism, ignorance, and poverty. The free form includes the parallelism of verbs and the juxtaposition of the present with the past. Black Americans are "never gaining, never reaping, never knowing and never understanding."[6] When religion faces reality, the contrast creates powerful reversal:

> For the boys and girls who grew in spite of these things to be
> man and woman, to laugh and dance and sing and play and
> drink their wine and religion and success, to marry their play-
> mates and bear children and then die of consumption and anemia
> and lynching.

Through biblical balance, "For My People" sets the white oppressor against the Black narrator. Social circumstance opposes racial and imaginative will, and disillusion opposes happiness. Blacks fashion a new world that encompasses many faces and people, "all the adams and eves and their countless generations." From the opening dedication (Stanza 1) to the final evocation (Stanza 10) the prophet-narrator speaks both as Christ and God. Ages ago, the Lord put His rainbow in the clouds. To the descendants of Noah it signified His promise that the world would never again end in flood. Human violence undermines biblical calm, as the first word repeats itself: "Let a new earth rise. Let another world be born. Let a bloody-peace be written in the sky. Let a second generation full of courage issue forth."

"We Have Been Believers," a visionary poem, juxtaposes Christianity with African conjure, and the Old Testament with the New, exemplified by St. John, St. Mark, and Revelation. The narrator ("we") represents the Black builders and singers in the past, for Walker seeks to interpret cultural signs. The theme is Black faith, first in Africa and then in America. As the verse shows movement from the past to the present, the ending combines Christianity and humanism. With extensive enjambment, the controlled rhapsody has a long first sentence, followed by indented ones that complete the meaning. The form literally typifies the Black American struggle. The long line is jolted because ending is illusory, and the reader renews his perusal just as the Black American continues the search for freedom. The narrator suggest the biblical scene in which death breaks the fifth seal (Revelation 6:11). There the prophet sees all the people who, slain in the service of God, wear garments as the narrator describes them.

The authenticating "we" is more focused than in either Ellison's *Invisible Man* or Baldwin's *Notes of a Native Son*. Their speakers are often educated and upwardly mobile people who move between white and Black American worlds. Walker's people on the contrary are frequently the secular and religious "folk" who share a communal quest. She blends historical sense with biblical implication: "Neither the slaver's whip nor the lyncher's rope nor the / bayonet could kill our black belief. In our hunger we / beheld the welcome table and in our nakedness the / glory of a long white robe." The narrator identifies Moloch, a god of cruel sacrifice, and all people who have died for no just cause. She prepares for the myth that dominates the last three parts of the poem, the miracle that Jesus performed on the eyes of a blind man. After He instructs him to wash them in the pool of Siloam, the man sees clearly (John 9:25). Another allusion suggests the miracle that Christ worked for the afflicted people near the Sea of Galilee. Walker's narrator knows the legend but awaits the transformation (Mark 7:37). The waiting prepares for an irony phrased in alliteration: "Surely the priests and the preachers and the powers will hear . . . / . . . now that our hands are empty and our hearts too full to pray." This narrator says that such people will send a sign—the biblical image of relief and redemption—but she implies something different. Although her humanism embraces Christianity, she adds militancy and impatience. Her rhetoric illustrates liquid sound, alliteration, and assonance: "We have been believers believing in our burdens and our / demigods too long. Now the needy no longer weep / and pray; the long-suffering arise, and our fists bleed / against the bars with a strange insistency."

The impatience pervades "Delta," which has the unifying type of the Twenty-third Psalm. Although the first part (ll. 1–35) presents the blood, corruption, and depression of the narrator's naturalistic world, the second (ll. 36–78) illustrates the restorative potential of nature. High mountain, river, orange, cotton, fern, grass, and onion share the promise. Dynamic fertility, the recleansed river (it flowed through swamps in the first part), can clear the Southern ground of sickness, rape, starvation, and ignorance. Water gives form to anger, yet thawing sets in. Coupled with liquidity, the loudness of thunder and cannon implies storm; the narrator compares the young girl to spring. Lovingly the speaker envisions vineyards, pastures, orchards, cattle, cotton, tobacco, and cane, "making us men in the fields we have tended / standing defending the land we have rendered rich and abiding and heavy with plenty." Interpreting the meaning of earth can help to bridge the distance between past decay and present maturity when the narrator celebrates the promise:

> the long golden grain for bread
> and the ripe purple fruit for wine
> the hills beyond the peace
> and the grass beneath for rest
> the music in the wind for us
> . . . .
> and the circling lines in the sky
> for dreams.

Elsewhere a gothic undercurrent and an allusion to Abel and Cain add complexity; so does an allusion to Christ and transubstantiation. Rhetorical power emerges because the harsh tone of the Old Testament threatens the merciful tone of the New one. Loosely plotted, the verse recounts the personal histories of the people in the valley. Still, the symbolical level dominates the literal one, and the poem portrays more deeply the human condition. The narrator profits from the gothicism which has influenced Ann Radcliffe, Charles Brockden Brown, and Edgar Allan Poe. Just as Walker's pictures create beauty for the African-American, they communicate a grace to all who appreciate symmetrical landscapes. The tension in her literary world comes from the romantic legacy of possibility set against denial: "High above us and round about us stand high mountains / rise the towering snowcapped mountains / while we are beaten and broken and bowed / here in this dark valley." Almost no rhyme scheme exists in the poem, but a predominance of three or four feet gives the impression of a very loose ballad. The fifth stanza of the second part has incremental repetition, as the undertone of Countee Cullen's poem "From the Dark Tower" heightens the deep despair, the paradox of desire and restraint: "We tend the crop and gather the harvest / but not for ourselves do we sweat and starve and spend . . . / here on this earth we dare not claim . . ." In the penultimate stanza the reader associates myth and history. While the narrator remembers the Blacks unrewarded in the Southern past, the imagery suggests Christ and transubstantiation. The speaker, however, alludes mainly to Abel slain by Cain (Genesis 4:10): "We with our blood have watered these fields / and they belong to us." Implicitly the promise of the Psalmist ("Yea though I walk through the valley of the shadow of death") has preceded.

In four quatrains, "Since 1619" strengthens Old Testament prefiguration. Aware of World War II, the narrator illuminates human blindness. She emphasizes the inevitability of death and the deterioration of world peace. With anaphora she repeats the Psalmist: "How many years . . . have I been singing Spirituals? / How long have I been praising God and shouting hallelujahs? / How long have I been hated and hating? / How long have I been living in hell for heaven?" She remembers the Valley of Dry Bones in which the Lord placed the prophet Ezekiel, whom He questioned if the bones could live. Whereas in the Bible salvation is external and divine, here the transformation comes from within. The poem contrasts moral renewal to the spiritual death during World War II and the pseudo-cleanliness of middle-class America.

Written in seven stanzas, "Today" has four lines in the first section and three in the second. Initially the poem portrays the ancient muse, the inspiration of all poetry, and later it illustrates poverty, fear, and sickness. Even the portrait of lynching cannot end the narrator's quest for cleanliness. Although Americans face death, they will continue to seek solace through intoxication and sex. The beginning of the poem foreshadows the end, but the directness in the second section supplants the general description in the first. The middle-class Americans in the first part have no bombing planes or air-raids to fear, yet they have masked violence and ethnocentric myth: "viewing weekly 'Wild West Indian and Shooting Sam,' 'Mama Loves Papa,' and 'Gone By the Breeze!'" Calories, eyemaline, henna rinse, and dental cream image a materialistic nation. With a deeper cleanliness, the speaker advises the reader within an ironic context: "Pray for second sight and the inner ear. Pray for bulwark against poaching patterns of dislocated days; pray for buttressing iron against insidious termite and beetle and locust and flies and lice and moth and rust and mold."

The religious types in the second and third sections of *For My People* rival neither those in the first section nor those in *Prophets for a New Day*. When Walker ignores biblical sources, often she vainly attempts to achieve cultural saturation.[7] Without biblical cadences her ballads frequently become average, if not monotonous. In "Yalluh Hammer," a folk poem about the "Bad Man," she manages sentimentality, impractical concern, and trickery, as a Black woman outsmarts the protagonist and steals his money.

But sometimes the less figurative sonnets are still boring.[8] "Childhood" lacks the condensation and focus to develop well the Petrarchan design. In the octave a young girl remembers workers who used to return home in the afternoons. Even during her maturity, the rags of poverty and the habitual grumbling color the Southern landscape still. Despite weaknesses, the poem suggests well a biblical analogue. The apostle Paul writes "When I was a child, I spake as a child: but when I became a man, I put away childish things" (I Corinthians 13:11). Walker's sonnet coincidentally begins, "When I was a child I knew red miners . . . / I also lived in a low cotton country . . . where sentiment and hatred still held sway / and only bitter land was washed away." The mature writer seeks now to restore and renew the earth.

In *Prophets* Walker illustrates some historical antitypes to the Old Testament. Her forms are the visionary poem, free verse sonnet, monody, pastoral, and gothic ballad in which she portrays freedom, speech, death, and rebirth. Her major images are fire, water, and wind. When she opposes marching to standing, the implied quest becomes metaphorical, for she recreates the human community in the spiritual wilderness. She looks beneath any typological concern of man's covenant with God, and even the pantheistic parallel of the Southerner's covenant with the land, to illuminate man's broken covenant with himself. The human gamut runs from death ("mourning bird")

to the potential of poetry ("humming bird"). Poetry recreates anthro-
pocentric space. The speaker depicts the breadth through dramatic
dialogue, sarcasm, and satire. Even the cold stone implies the poten-
tial for creative inspiration or Promethean fire. The narrator verbally
paints urban corruption in the bitter cold and frozen water. Her por-
trait images not only the myth of fragmentation and dissolution, but
the courage necessary to confront and transcend them. Her world
is doubly Southern. Here the Old South still withstands Northern
invasion, but the Black South endures both. One attains the mythi-
cal building beyond (compare Thomas Wolfe), the human house,
through fire. Form is imagined silence. Poetry, both catharsis and
purgation, parallels speaking, crying, and weaving. The center in-
cludes geometric space and aesthetic beauty. To portray anthropo-
centric depth is to clarify the significance of human cleansing.

Although the sonnets and ballads in *For My People* are weak, the
typological poems in *Prophets for a New Day* envision universal free-
dom. But neither Walker nor her reader can remain at visionary
heights, for the real world includes the white hood and fiery cross.
Even the latter image fails to save the poem "Now," in which the sub-
ject is civil rights. Here both images of place and taste imply filth,
as doors, dark alleys, balconies, and washrooms reinforce moral in-
dignation. The Klan marks "Kleagle with a Klux / and a fiery burn-
ing cross." Yet awkward rhythms have preceded. In shifting from three
feet to four, the speaker stumbles: "In the cleaning room and closets /
with the washrooms . . . / . . . marked 'For Colored Only.'" The ear
of "Sit-ins" catches more sharply the translation of the Bible into
history. Written in twelve lines of free verse, the lyric depicts the stu-
dents at North Carolina A & T University, who in 1960 sat down
at the counter of a dime store and began the Civil Rights Movement.
The speaker recreates Southern history. In the shining picture, the
reader sees the Angel Michael who drove Adam and Eve from Para-
dise, but the portrait becomes more secular: "With courage and faith,
convictions and intelligence / The first to blaze a flaming path for
justice / And awaken consciences / Of these stony ones." The im-
plement that in the Bible and Milton symbolized Paradise Lost be-
comes a metaphor for Paradise Regained. In viewpoint the narrator
gives way to the demonstrators themselves: "*Come, Lord Jesus, Bold
Young Galilean / Sit Beside This Counter, Lord, With Me.*"

As with most of Walker's antitypical poems, "Sit-Ins" hardly rivals
"Ballad of the Free," one of her finest. The latter work portrays the

heroic missions and tragic deaths of slave insurrectionists and excels through consistent rhythm as well as compression of image. At first the verse seems true to the title. Although the design of the typical ballad usually emphasizes a rhythmic contrast between two lines in succession, "Ballad of the Free," stresses a contrast between whole stanzas. Of the twelve sections which comprise the poem, each of the four quatrains follows a tercet which serves as the refrain. The narrator adds a striking twist to St. Matthew (19:30; 20:16), in which Peter asks Jesus what will happen to people who have forsaken everything to follow Him. Christ replies that the social status will be reversed. Although He speaks about the beginning of the apocalypse in which all persons are judged, Walker's narrator forsees the end of the apocalypse in which all are equal: "The serpent is loosed and the hour is come. . . ."

The refrain balances social history and biblical legend. The first stanza presents Nat Turner, the leader of the slave insurrection in South Hampton, Virginia, during 1831. After the first refrain, the reader recognizes Gabriel Prosser, whom a storm once forced to suspend a slave revolt in Richmond, Virginia. With a thousand other slaves, Prosser planned an uprising that collapsed in 1800. Betrayed by fellow bondsmen, he and fifteen others were hanged on October 7 of that year. After the first echo of the refrain, Denmark Vesey, who enlisted thousands of Blacks for an elaborate slave plot in Charleston, S.C., and the vicinity appears in the fifth stanza. Authorities arrested 131 Blacks and four whites, and when the matter was settled, thirty-seven people were hanged. Toussaint L'Ouverture, who at the turn of the eighteenth and nineteenth centuries liberated Haitian slaves, follows the second echo of the refrain. Shortly afterward an evocation of John Brown intensifies the balance between history and sound. With thirteen Whites and five Blacks, Brown attacked Harper's Ferry on October 16, 1859, and by December 2 of that year, he was also hanged. In the poem, as in the Southern past, the death of the rebel is foreshadowed. Gifted with humane vision, he wants to change an inegalitarian South. But those who maintain the status quo will kill, so the hero becomes the martyr.

In order to emphasize Turner as historical paradigm, the narrator ignores the proper chronology of L'Ouverture, Prosser, Vesey, Turner, and Brown. She gives little of the historical background but calls upon the names of legend. What does she achieve, by naming her last hero, if not a symmetry of color? The ballad that began with Black Nat

Turner ends with White John Brown, for if action alone determines a basis for fraternity, racial distinction is insignificant.

For a central portrait of Turner, the verse moves backward and forward in both typological and apocalyptic time. As with the narrator of Hughes's "Negro Speaks of Rivers," the speaker can comprehend different decades. Because she is outside of Time, L'Ouverture and Brown, who come from different periods, appear to her with equal clarity. Until the eleventh stanza, the biblical sureness of the refrain has balanced history. The note of prophecy sounds in the slowness and firmness of racial progress: "*Wars and Rumors of Wars have gone, / But Freedom's army marches on. / The heroes' list of dead is long, / And Freedom still is for the strong.*" The narrator recalls Christ (Mark 13:7) who prophesies wars and rumors of war, but foretells salvation for endurers. The final refrain interfuses with the fable and history: "The serpent is loosed and the hour is come."

"At the Lincoln Monument in Washington, August 28, 1963" presents analogues to Isaiah, Exodus, Genesis, and Deuteronomy. Written in two stanzas, the poem has forty-four lines. The speaker dramatizes chronicle through biblical myth, racial phenomenology, and Judaeo-Christian consciousness. She advances superbly from the participant to the interpreter, but even the latter speaks from within an aesthetic mask. The poetic vision authenticates the morality of her fable and the biblical analogue. The first stanza has twenty-eight lines, and the second has sixteen. As the speaker recalls the march on Washington, in which more than 250,000 people demonstrated for civil rights, she attributes to Martin Luther King, Jr., the leader of the movement, the same rhetorical art she now remembers him by. The analogue is Isaiah: "The grass withereth, the flower fadeth: but the word of our God shall stand for ever" (40:8). Two brothers, according to the fable, led the Israelites out of Egypt.[9] Sentences of varied length complement the juxtaposition of cadences which rise and fall. The narrator names neither King as "Moses" nor King's youthful follower as "Aaron," yet she clarifies a richness of oration and implies the heroic spirit. King, before his death, said that he had been to the mountain top and that he had seen the Promised Land. But the speaker retraces the paradigm of the life literarily; she distills the love of the listeners who saw him and were inspired: "There they stand . . . / Old man with a dream he has lived to see come true."

Although the first eleven lines of the poem are descriptive, the twelfth combines chronicle and prefiguration. The speaker projects the social present into the mythical past. Her words come from a Civil Rights song, "We Woke Up One Morning With Our Minds Set On Freedom." The social activist wants the immediate and complete liberation which the rhetorician (speaker and writer) translates into literary symbol: "We woke up one morning in Egypt / And the river ran red with blood . . . / And the houses of death were afraid."

She remembers, too, the story of Jacob, who returns home with his two wives, Leah and Rachel (Genesis 30:25–43). Laban, the father-in-law, gave him speckled cattle, but now the narrator understands that Jacob's "*house* [Africa-America] has grown into a Nation. The slaves break forth from bondage" (emphasis mine). In Old Testament fashion, she cautions against fatigue in the pursuit of liberty. Through heightened style, she becomes a prophet whose medium is eternal language. She has mastered alliteration, assonance, and resonance.

> Write this word upon your hearts
> And mark this message on the doors of your houses
> See that you do not forget
> How this day the Lord has set our faces toward Freedom
> Teach these words to your children
> And see that they do not forget them.

Walker's poetry alludes subtly to King but refers to Malcolm X directly. The verse dedicated to Malcolm portrays him as Christ. Nearly a Petrarchan sonnet, the poem has several lines of four or six feet instead of the expected five-foot line. Even a concession of off-rhyme does not make a Petrarchan scheme unfold. The comments sound repetitious because they are. As with the earlier sonnet "Child-hood," "Malcolm" appears at first to deserve oblivion because here, too, Walker fails to condense and control metrics. Still, the quiet appeal is clear. The Christ story compels rereading. When Malcolm is associated with a dying swan in the octave, the narrator alludes to the Ovidian legend of the beautiful bird which sings just before death.[10] Malcolm takes on Christ's stigmata: "Our blood and water pour from your flowing wounds."

Vivid and noble portraits of crucifixion, another type of martyr-dom, give even more vitality to "For Andy Goodman, Michael Schwer-ner, and James Chaney" (hereafter, "For Andy"), a poem about three Civil Rights workers murdered in Mississippi on June 21, 1964. The elegy complements the seasonal and diurnal cycle through the reaffirmation of human growth and spiritual redemption. Despite the questionable value of martyrdom, sunrise balances sunset, and beautiful leaves partly compensate for human mutilation. In dramatic reversal, Walker's narrator uses the literary technique which distinguishes *Lycidas, Adonais,* and *When Lilacs Last in the Dooryard Bloom'd.*

The flower and the paradigmatic bird (lark, robin, mourning bird, bird of sorrow, bird of death) restore both an epic and elegaic mood. The reader half-hears the echo of the goddess Venus who mourns for Adonis, as *mourning* and *morning,* excellent puns, signify the cycle and paradox of life. [11] The short rhythm, two feet, and the longer rhythm, three or four, provide the solemn folksiness of a very loose ballad or free verse. With interior rhyme, the musical balance communicates quiet pathos: "They have killed these three. / They have killed them for me." The gentle suggestion of the trinity, the tragic flight of the bird, and the slow but cyclical turning from spring to spring intensify the narrator's sadness and grief.

Just as "For Andy" shows Walker's grace of style, the title poem of *Prophets* illustrates that the Bible prefigures the eloquence. As with the earlier poem "Delta," "Prophets" resists paraphrase because it portrays Black American history abstractly. The poem has three parts. The first shows that the Word which came to the biblical prophets endures, and the next represents the actual appearance of the ancient vision to new believers. In the third part, the reader moves to a final understanding about tragic death. While the poet marks the recurrence of sacred light, fire, gentleness, and artistic speech, she contrasts White and Black, dark and light, age and youth, life and death. Some allusions to Ezekiel and Amos now fuse with others from Ecclesiastes and Isaiah. Amos tells of a prophet-priest of sixth century B.C., a watchman over the Israelites during the exile in Babylon, by the river of Cheber (Ezek. 1:15-20). As a herdsman from the southern village of Tekoa, Judah, he went to Bethel in Samaria to preach a religion of social justice and righteousness. He attacked economic exploitation and privilege and criticized the priests who stressed ritual above justice. Because Amos is Walker's personal symbol of Martin Luther King, Jr., she provides more background about him than about others. The reader knows his name, character, and homeland.

But Walker reinvigorates the scriptures socially and historically. She is no eighteenth-century Jupiter Hammon who rewrites the Bible without any infusion of personal suffering. She feels strongly and personally that the demonstrators in the sixties antitypify the Scriptures: "So today in the pulpits and the jails, /. . . A fearless shepherd speaks at last / To his suffering weary sheep." She implies perseverance even in the face of death, and her speaker blends the images of the New Testament with those from *Beowulf*. Her lines depict the beast:

> His mark is on the land.
> His horns and his hands and his lips are gory with our blood.
> He is Death and Destruction and Trouble
> And he walks in our houses at noonday
> And devours our defenders at midnight.

The literary word images fear and sacrifice more than immediate redemption. What shadows the fate of the good? The beast

> has crushed them with a stone.
> He drinks our tears for water
> And he drinks our blood for wine;
> He eats our flesh like a ravenous lion
> And he drives us out of the city
> To be stabbed on a lonely hill.

The same scene relives the crucifixion.

Walker draws heavily upon the Bible for typological unity. Of the twenty-two poems in *Prophets*, seven of the last nine have biblical names for titles, including "Jeremiah," "Isaiah," "Amos-1963," "Amos (Postscript-1968)," "Joel," "Hosea," and "Micah." A similar problem besets all of them, though to a different extent. The aesthetic response relies on historical sense more than on dramatized language, and passing time will weaken the emotional hold. In "Jeremiah," the narrator is conscious of both the fallen world and the apocalyptic one. She suggests Benjamin Mays, who has been a preacher and educator in Atlanta for over fifty years. Seeking to lift the "curse" from the land, Mays wants to redeem the corrupted city. The mythical denotation of the place — "Atalanta" — inspires the cultural imagination. Once a girl by that name lost a race to Hippomenes, her suitor, because she digressed from her course to pursue golden apples.[12] Yet Walker's poem does more than oppose Mays to urban materialism. Through his articulation (the spoken word), he signifies the artist and the writer. The narrator who recounts the tale is an artist, too, since Walker's speakers and heroes mirror each other. Although Jeremiah appears as a contemporary man, he exists in a half-way house between legend and reality. Despite limitations, the final six lines of the verse combine myth and anaphora, where the speaker compares the imaginative and historical worlds more closely than elsewhere. Once destroyed by fire, the current Atlanta suggests Babylon, capital first of Babylonia and then of Chaldea on the Euphrates river. As the scene of the biblical Exile, the city represents grandeur and wickedness. The book of Psalms portrays the despair of the Israelites who sat down and wept when they remembered Zion. With an undertone of an old folk ballad, Walker builds a literary vision. While anaphora strengthens solemnity, the voice subsumes both narrator and prophet:

> My God we are still here. We are still down here Lord,
> Working for a kingdom of Thy Love.
> We weep for this city and for this land
> We weep for Judah and beloved Jerusalem
> O Georgia! "Where shall you stand in the Judgment?"

Through the fire, the mark, and the word, "Isaiah" clarifies the typology which leads from "Lincoln Monument," midway through the volume, to "Elegy" at the end. Jeremiah expresses himself in the public forum as well as on television. He resembles Adam Clayton Powell, Jr., a major Civil Rights activist in Harlem during the depression. Powell persuaded many Harlem businesses, including Harlem Hospital, to hire Blacks. As chairman of the Coordinating Committee on Employment, he led a demonstration which forced the World's Fair to adopt a similar policy in 1939. He desegregated many congressional facilities, Washington restaurants, and theaters. He proposed first the witholding of federal funds from projects which showed racial discrimination; he introduced the first legislation to desegregate the armed forces; he established the right of Black journalists to sit in the press galleries of the United States House of Representatives and in the Senate. As chairman of the House Committee on Education and Labor in 1960, he supported forty-eight pieces of legislation on social welfare and later earned a letter of gratitude from President Johnson.

In 1967, however, Powell's House colleagues raised charges of corruption and financial mismanagement against him. In January he was stripped of his chairmanship and barred from the House, pending an investigation. On March 1, 1967 Powell was denied a seat in the House by a vote of 307 to 116, despite the committee's recommendation that he only be censured, fined, and placed at the bottom of the seniority list. On April 11 a special election was held to fill Powell's seat. Powell, who was not campaigning and was on the Island of Bimini and who could not even come to New York City because of a court judgment against him in a defamation case, received 74% of the Harlem vote cast.[13]

Even more clearly, the "Amos" poems reconfirm Walker's greater metaphor for Martin Luther King, Jr. The first of these two verses, twenty lines in length, portrays Amos as a contemporary shepherd who preaches in the depths of Alabama and elsewhere: "standing in the Shadow of our God / Tending his flocks all over the hills of Albany / And the seething streets of Selma and of bitter Birmingham." As with the first "Amos" poem, the second ("Postscript — 1968") is written in free verse. With only ten lines, however, the latter is shorter. King, the prophet of justice, appears through the fluidity and the wholesomeness of the "O" sound: "From Montgomery to Memphis he marches / He stands on the threshold of tomorrow / He breaks the bars of iron and they remove the signs / He opens the gates of our prisons."

Many of the short poems that follow lack the high quality found in some of Walker's other typological lyrics. "Joel" uses the standard free verse, but the historical allusion is obscure. "Hosea" suffers from the same problem. The Bible presents the figure as having an unfaithful wife, but Walker's poem presents a Hosea who, marked for death, writes love letters to the world. Is the man Eldridge Cleaver? The letters and the theme of redemption clearly suggest him, but one can never be sure. The legend could better suit the man. The last poem in *Prophets* benefits appropriately from some of Walker's favorite books such as Ecclesiastes, Isaiah, and St. John. "Elegy," a verse in two parts, honors the memory of Manford Kuhn, professor and friend. Summer and sunshine give way to winter snow and "frothy wood," since the green harvest must pass. But art forms ironically preserve themselves through fire, and engraving comes from corrosion. Eternity depends paradoxically upon decay. The first section concerns the cycle of nature which continually turns; the second, an elaborate conceit, depicts people as ephemeral artists. Reminiscent of Vergil's *Aeneid*, Shelley's "The Witch of Atlas," and Danner's short lyric, "The Slave and the Iron Lace," Walker's second section begins:

> Within our house of flesh we weave a web of time
> Both warp and woof within the shuttle's clutch
> In leisure and in haste no less a tapestry
> Rich pattern of our lives.
> The gold and scarlet intertwine
> Upon our frame of dust an intricate design. . . .

Here are her ablest statement and restatement of the iamb. The "I" sound supports assonance and rhyme, even though the poem is basically free. At first the idea of human transitoriness reinforces *Ecclesiastes* which powerfully presents the theme. In a second look, however, one traces the thought to Isaiah (40:7): "The grass withereth, the flower fadeth: because the spirit of the Lord bloweth upon it." But the speaker knows the ensuing verse equally well: "The grass withereth, the flower fadeth; but the *word* [emphasis mine] of our God shall stand for ever" (40:8). Poetry, an inspired creation in words, is divine as well. To the extent that Kuhn showed Christ-like love and instruction for his students, his spirit transcends mortality. For any who demonstrate similar qualities is the vision any less true and universal? To Nicodemus, the Pharisee whom Jesus told to be reborn (John 3:8), the final allusion belongs.

> We live again
> In children's faces, and the sturdy vine
> Of daily influences: the prime
> Of teacher, neighbor, student, and friend
> All merging on the elusive wind.   (33–37)

Patient nobility becomes the poet who has recreated Martin Luther King, Jr., as Amos. She has kept the neatly turned phrase of Countee Cullen but replaced Tantalus and Sisyphus with Black students and sit-ins. For her literary fathers, she reaches back to the nineteenth-century prophets Blake, Byron, Shelley, and Tennyson. Her debt extends no less to Walt Whitman and to Langston Hughes, for her predecessor is any poet who forsees a new paradise and who portrays the coming. As with Hughes, Walker is a romantic. But Hughes had either to subordinate his perspective to history, or to ignore history almost completely, and to speak less about events than about personal and racial symbols. Walker, on the contrary, equally combines events and legends but reaffirms the faith of the spirituals. Although her plots sometimes concern murder, her narrators reveal an image of racial freedom and human peace. The best of her imagined South prefigures the future.

NOTES

1. See Paula Giddings, "Some Themes in the Poetry of Margaret Walker," *Black World* (Dec. 1971), 20–34. Although it fails to emphasize the importance of literary form, the essay gives a general impression of historical background and literary tradition.

2. See Margaret Walker and Nikki Giovanni, *A Poetic Equation: Conversations* (Washington, D.C.: Howard Univ. Press, 1974), 56. Through logic Walker has the better of the friendly argument.

3. Charles H. Rowell, "Poetry, History, and Humanism" (interview), *Black World*, 25 (Dec. 1975), 4–17; Arthur P. Davis, "Margaret Walker," in *From the Dark Tower: Afro-American Writers 1900 to 1960* (Washington, D.C.: Howard Univ. Press, 1974), 180–85.

4. Poems mentioned, other than those by Walker, are available in Dudley Randall, *The Black Poets* (New York: Bantam, 1971).

5. See Joseph Greenborg, *Language Typology* (The Hague: Mouton, 1974); Paul J. Korshin, "The Development of Abstracted Typology in England, 1650–1820," in *Literary Uses of Typology*, ed. Earl Miner (Princeton: Princeton Univ. Press, 1977); Mason I. Lawrance, "Introduction," *The Figures or Types of the Old Testament* (New York: Johnson, 1969); Roland Bartel, "The Bible in Negro Spirituals," in ibid.; Sacvan Bercovitch, *Typology and American Literature* (Amherst: Univ. of Massachusetts Press, 1972); Emory Elliott, "From Father to Son," in *Literary Uses*, ed. Miner; Theodore Ziolkowski, "Some Features of Religious Figuralism in Twentieth Century Literature," in *Literary Uses*, ed. Miner; Ursula Brumm, *American Thought and Religious Typology* (New Brunswick, N.J.: Rutgers Univ. Press, 1970).

6. Primary texts used are Margaret Walker, *For My People* (New Haven: Yale Univ. Press, 1977) and Margaret Walker, *Prophets for a New Day* (Detroit: Broadside, 1970).

7. See Stephen Henderson, *Understanding the New Black Poetry* (New York: William Morrow, 1973), 62–66.

8. Reviewers disagree about the form in which Walker succeeds most ably. See Elizabeth Drew, *Atlantic*, 170 (Dec. 1942), 10; Arna Bontemps, *Christian Science Monitor* (Nov. 14, 1942), 690; Louis Untermeyer, *Yale Review* (Winter 1943), 370. All discuss *For My People*. Drew praises the experimentation in rhythmical language. Bontemps says that the ballads and sonnets show a folk understanding, but he comments less about their literary success. The reviewer in *New Republic*, on the contrary, finds the sonnets to be weak but the ballads to be strong. Untermeyer praises Walker's success

in winning the prize in the Yale series (a first for a Black) but discovers flaws in both the sonnets and ballads.

9. See Exodus, 4:14–17, 7:8–12, 32:1–6; Numbers, 17:1–11, 20:12–29.

10. Ovid, *Metamorphoses* (Baltimore: Penguin Books, 1961), 322.

11. Ibid., 244.

12. Ibid., 240–44. See the brilliant analysis in W.E.B. Du Bois, *The Souls of Black Folk* (1961; rpt. New York: New American Library, 1969), 117–20. The volume was published originally in 1903.

13. Peter M. Bergman and Mort N. Bergman, *The Chronological History of the Negro in America* (New York: New American Library, 1969), 354–55.

Harry B. Shaw

Perceptions of Men in the Early Works of Gwendolyn Brooks

Gwendolyn Brooks is a premier portraitist of Black men and of Black women. Yet, to my knowledge, no one has looked specifically at Gwendolyn Brooks's treatment of Black men in her works. Arthur P. Davis comes closest in his articles entitled "Gwendolyn Brooks: Poet of the Unheroic" and "The Black-and-Tan Motif in the Poetry of Gwendolyn Brooks."[1] George E. Kent, in "The Poetry of Gwendolyn Brooks," reveals that she is a poet of the Black experience and therefore is adept at incisive portraiture of the wide variety of Black men and women in the urban setting.[2] In "The Women of Bronzeville" Beverly Guy-Sheftall discusses Brooks's treatment of urban Black women and thereby casts reflective light on the poet's treatment of Black men.[3] Whether Brooks's images of Black men are reflected in her portraits of women or presented in their own light, the images are always seen from the perspective of a woman.[4] Her personae's points of view most often involve an omniscient observer who closely identifies with or at least thoroughly understands the Black men presented in her works.

In light of this perspective, an examination of Brooks's treatment of men would fit logically among and also supplement other analyses of the treatment of Black men in the works of Black women writers. Brooks's works published between 1940 and 1960 — specifically, *A Street in Bronzeville, Annie Allen, Maud Martha,* and *The Bean Eaters* — lend themselves particularly well to a discussion of Brooks's depictions of men in the everyday urban setting. Brooks presents good pictures of the Black man as hero progressing and retrogressing in the various stages of the Black experience as he tries to cope with his environment. These depictions are arranged into several discernible, though not mutually exclusive, categories, including the citizen in relation to the larger society, the family member in relation to the personae and to the reader, and the love object.

As citizens, the Black men in Brooks's works most often reveal their relationship to the larger society as patriots fighting the nation's wars or espousing its causes, or as victims of the oppression and deceit encountered in the larger society. With a necessary dualness of character similar to that which haunts the Black artist, the Black citizen seeks a reliable and positive relationship to the larger society.[5] Miss Brooks, through her images of the Black man as citizen, constantly points out the paradoxes that abound in the disparity between the American creed and the American reality.

Even as patriot, the Black man experiences the tension of being torn between the comfort of the freedom to pursue the American dream and the pain of the necessity to escape the American reality which denies fulfillment of that dream. The tension between the American dream and the American reality presents a negative dialectic that results in confusion and vacillation for the Black citizen between allegiance and repudiation. The energy which drives the dialectic is the quest for fulfillment of the dream, the perceived birthright of all American citizens.

Such a quest is readily apparent in "Negro Hero." Here a Black man, who suggests Dorie Miller, the Black hero of Pearl Harbor, summarizes the dilemma faced by the Black man who would be a patriot. The poem shows the Black would-be patriot contemplating his paradoxical encounter with the organized opposition to the advancement of Black men toward fulfilling their concept of manhood.

A brief account of the heroism and its historical context illuminates Brooks's treatment of the Black man as hero in this poem. Dorie Miller, the first Black American hero of World War II, was a Navy messman at the time of the Japanese attack on Pearl Harbor in 1941. Without previous experience, Miller manned a machine gun and shot down four enemy planes.[6] At that time the armed forces were strictly segregated, making it illegal for Miller to man the guns. Although Miller received the Navy Cross, many critics of Black soldiers insisted that they were incapable of participating efficiently in modern warfare.[7] Hence, the opening stanza:

> I had to kick their law into their teeth in order to save them.
> However I have heard that sometimes you have to deal
> Devilishly with drowning men in order to swim them to shore.
> Or they will haul themselves and you to the trash and the fish
>   beneath.

> (When I think of this, I do not worry about a few
> Chipped Teeth.)[8]

The irony of the war situation itself is equaled, if not surpassed, by that of the condescending mentality of the American public. The very glory of the news as it was received "in the Caucasian dailies / As well as the Negro weeklies" becomes a source of irony for Black people. ("They are not concerned that it was hardly the Enemy / My fight was against / But them.")

In the reflection on the news coverage, the mild sarcasm of the persona becomes evident with the repetition of "of course" in the third stanza. Even in an act of heroism, the Black man was denied his full accord as a man:

> Of course all the delicate rehearsal shots of my childhood
>   massed in mirage before me
> Of course I was child
> And my first swallow of the liquor of battle bleeding black
>   air dying and demon noise
> Made me wild.   (pp. 32–33)

The implication is that whereas a white soldier performing similar feats would have been described as manly, the Black man's acts are attributed to "blood . . . boiling about in my head," "my boy itch," "shots of my childhood," and "of course" to being a child wild with the first taste of battle.

The persona's incisiveness in the fourth stanza presents the soldier's acrid assessment of the risks he knowingly took while revealing yet another irony in the multilayered insult — that he is aware of the depravity of those who seek to dehumanize him:

> Their white-gowned democracy was my fair lady.
> With her knife lying cold, straight, in the softness of
>   her sweet-flowing sleeve.   (p. 33)

The emphasis is on contrasting the boy-animal image of the third stanza with that of a man, perhaps a bigger-than-life man, fighting the enemy within as much as the enemy without:

> It was kinder than that, though, and I showed like a banner
>   my kindness.
> I loved. And a man will guard when he loves.

The fifth and sixth stanzas deal with the ambivalence of the Black man who would be patriot in the face of American duplicity as well as abject racism.

> Still—am I good enough to die for them, is my blood bright
>   enough to be spilled,
> Was my constant back-question—are they clear
> On this? Or do I intrude even now?   (p. 33)

The personification of "white-gowned democracy" as an object of love helps in the interpretation of another poem about the would-be Black patriot during a war. The ambivalence—the "constant back-question"—and the irony continue apace. The very title, "Love Note I: Surely," again suggests a possible continuation of the theme and the technique. It is ironic that here the Black man utters an expression of doubt in a poem entitled "Surely." Although the multiplicity of possible referents in the poem lends itself to a display of artful ambiguity, the persona can be seen using the lover motif to suggest the relationship between Black people and their country. The sestet of the sonnet helps to unravel some of the ambiguity of the octave. Read negatively, in light of the sestet, "surely" becomes an expression of doubt rather than certainty. Like the repetition of "of course" in "Negro Hero," the use of "surely" in this poem focuses the sarcasm on that about which the Black man would be most secure. Surely the country and its democracy could not be thought of by the Black man as "mine"; surely to him country had not been "all honest, lofty as a cloud"; surely he would not be assured of the country's love; and surely the country's eyes were not "ungauzed."[9]

"Love Note II: Flags" is another sonnet from the same series as "Love Note I: Surely." As in "Negro Hero" and "Love Note I: Surely," "Love Note II: Flags" continues the motif of the unrequited lover to convey the Black soldier's disillusionment over his country's failure to champion his cause in his war for dignity. Democracy is alluded to here as a lady whose flag the Black fox-hole soldier carries. Bitter about being whimsically jilted by the fair lady of democracy, the soldier makes a sarcastic proposition in the octave:

> I pull you down my foxhole. Do you mind?
> You burn in bits of saucy color then.
> I let you flutter out against the pained
> Volleys. Against my power crumpled and wan.   (p. 58)

"Dear defiance" suggests the indignation provoked whenever the flag and what it represents are invoked by Black people to champion their cause. The soldier's digust is shown by his dragging the flag into the foxhole with him and asking derisively, "Do you mind?"

Other poems about the Black man as soldier-patriot, such as "The White Troops Had Their Orders but the Negroes Looked Like Men" and "The Progress," reveal as much about the societal mentality against which Black people struggle as about Black people themselves. The poems depicting the Black man attempting to be a patriot reveal the tension caused by the attraction and the danger of committing to the American dream. Indeed the danger is sufficient to transform the Black citizen who would be a patriot into a victim of the larger society. To be sure, each of the patriots discussed so far has been a victim of racism in the larger society. The Negro hero, for example, was a victim of racism before as well as after his heroic moment. Most often, however, Black people who are victims of the larger society are not soldiers or patriots but ordinary citizens of the ghetto. They share, though, the same flirtation with the American dream as do the would-be patriots. The notion of being able to obtain the good life—or some aspects of it—provides the lure which eventually traps Black people as victims of society.

Rudolph Reed of "The Ballad of Rudolph Reed" also pursues the American dream on the home front and falls victim to the larger society. Prompted by the new wave of integration in the North's "Promised Land," Reed and his family move into a house in a white neighborhood. Although the "oaken" Reed tries to endure the ensuing violence, he is forced to retaliate with his own violence. Shortly after attacking the mob, he is killed by his neighbors who kick his corpse and call him "Nigger." Reed is clearly the victim of racism and in his resistance to it assumes an almost larger-than-life stature reminiscent of Dorie Miller. Like Miller, he risks his life for an ideal and chooses to preserve the human spirit at all costs rather than to subdue it for the sake of material wealth or even physical well-being. Reed's deliberately pressing the hand of his wife indicates that both Reed and his wife are aware of the necessity for him to face the white mob. The courage and resolve with which he goes knowingly to his death make him both hero and *pharmakos* or scapegoat victim.[10] The persona clearly does not view Rudolph Reed as the "Nigger" villain whose corpse is to be kicked and cursed for transgression of the larger society's notion of "place." Rather, the persona has already exalted his manhood by calling him "oaken as a man could be."

Other victims who fit the *pharmakos* mode of the persecuted Black people are Sammy in "The Ballad of Pearl May Lee" and the Dark Villain in "A Bronzeville Mother Loiters in Mississippi. Meanwhile, a Mississippi Mother Burns Bacon." Both of these Black men become victims for violating the boundaries of their "place" as conceived by the larger society. Sammy is victim of the larger society's taboo concerning sex involving a Black man and a white woman. The penalty is death. Again the poet presents a situation in which capricious pursuit of the dream is disastrous. In this case the trap is literally set for the victim whose crime is his weakness. Although the woman had enticed him to have sex with her, it was he who by formula was to be society's victim. Pearl May Lee knew that Sammy was society's victim in more than one way. To her he was already spiritually dead, having suffered, according to Arthur P. Davis, "a spiritual mutilation as real as the physical one he suffers at the hands of the mob."[11]

"A Bronzeville Mother Loiters in Mississippi. Meanwhile, a Mississippi Mother Burns Bacon" presents the story of the lynching of Emmett Till, a fourteen-year-old Black Chicago youth who had been visiting relatives in Mississippi and allegedly made improper advances toward a white woman (the mock heroine of the poem). By contrast to Rudolph Reed, who knows full well the dire consequences of his retaliation, Emmett Till's innocence is emphasized in the thoughts of the "heroine": "He should have been older, perhaps" (p. 318). The point is that whether the transgression is done in innocence or awareness, the old formula holds true in making the Black person the scapegoat victim of American society.

"A Man of the Middle Class" exemplifies another aspect of the lure and the trap involved in the pursuit of the American dream. Even when the Black person falls victim to the larger society for reasons other than racism as illustrated in this poem, there is the suggestion of an obscure, ironic but definite danger in capricious pursuit of the dream. The message seems to be that it is better not to lose sight of one's identity, values, and roots, as suggested by "I am bedraggled, with sundry dusts to be shed; / Trailing desperate tarnished tassels" (p. 334). These dusts and tassels hint at the unwelcome past. He, like Dorie Miller and the other soldier-patriots, has pursued the dream, and, also like the patriots, he falls victim to the foibles of the American system. Although he is materially successful, he still lacks answers. He contemplates the solution that suicide brings to the "executives . . . copied long ago" (p. 340). The implication is that unhealthy pursuit of the dream can lead to extreme materialism and spiritual depravation that results in their taking their own lives in despair.

Because fulfillment of the American dream for Black people is fraught with illusions and pitfalls, many Blacks choose the relative physical and spiritual safety of pursuing a perverted, innocuous, non-competitive alteration of the dream or of abandoning dreams altogether. Satin-Legs Smith in "The Sundays of Satin-Legs Smith" is somewhat like the man of the middle class in his need to shed what he considers to be his seamy past. Hence, "he sheds with his pajamas, shabby days." The persona further reminds the reader of Satin-Legs's plainer past:

> . . . cabbage and pigtails,
> Old intimacy with alleys, garbage pails,
> Down in the deep (but always beautiful) South
> Where roses blush their blithest (it is said)
> And sweet magnolias put Chanel to shame.   (p. 27)

Satin-Legs camouflages his impotence with the finest clothes and doting women. Avoiding any association with the "straight tradition," which reminds him by contrast of his own impotence and spiritual death, he convinces himself that he is royal and fine. Having to live the life of illusion while shunning his own identity, he is a subtle victim of the larger society that denies him free access to the American dream.

Others denied the dream include the seven pool players at the Golden Shovel in "We Real Cool" and Lester after seeing the western movie "Strong Men Riding Horses." The young men at the pool hall are clearly victims to the extent that they have relinquished whatever hopes they may have had in order to be "cool," exemplifying the "live-fast, die-young pattern of many urban black youths."[12] In a related poem, "Strong Men Riding Horses," Lester is so victimized by the larger society that he deprecates his weakness in contrast to the strong white men in the western. Feeling vastly inferior to the white men, Lester remarks, "I am not like that. I pay rent, am addled / By illegible landlords, run, if robbers call" (p. 313).

The Black people who are depicted as victims of the larger society may be quite different from each other in circumstances, in the methods of their victimization, and in their reactions to these methods. A common thread in their victimization, however, is society's denial of their manhood and its alienation of them from the normal pursuit of the American dream. Given Brooks's awareness of and attention to the pervasiveness of racism in America, it is plausible that all of the Black male citizens depicted in her works could to some extent be seen as victims of the larger society. Just as it has already been evidenced that Brooks's early poetry is conducive to the perception of the Black man as patriot, it is also worthwhile to view these Black men from yet other perspectives as well in order to appreciate them as complex, three-dimensional figures.

In several of Brooks's poems the Black man is clearly perceived as a member of a family—whether the family is societal or biological. De Witt Williams, for instance, can be perceived as belonging to the American Black family. In "Of De Witt Williams on His Way To Lincoln Cemetery" the repeated reference to "plain black boy" suggests an archetypal Black man who belonged collectively to all Black people. According to Eugene Redmond, "De Witt's journey is the black American (South to North) odyssey depicted by Wright, Baldwin, Claude Brown, and company."[13] As a representative black man, De Witt is shown to have frequented the places and to have indulged in activities common to an urban Black man—the pool hall, the show, Forty-seventh Street, underneath the L, the dance halls, his women, and his liquid joy. The refrain of "Swing low swing low sweet sweet chariot" taps the folk spiritual reservoir that is the common heritage of all Black people.

Another Black Everyman figure is Satin-Legs Smith. He, too, is presented with obvious linkage to the Black folk tradition and to the South, but, unlike De Witt Williams, he tries to deny them. At times, however, the "plain black boy" image forces its way to the surface as the reader is reminded of a side of Satin-Legs's life that is somewhat seamier than the one he would display to himself and to others. Flowers remind Satin-Legs of death mainly because they remind him of his past—of his real self—and as he listens to the vendor singing the blues, Satin-Legs once again is reminded of his past; the reader then realizes why it is unlikely for Satin-Legs to have an affinity for flowers or classical musicians or to accept the "straight tradition." As a creature of his ancestors, Satin-Legs reveals the influence of the Black familial experience:

The pasts of his ancestors lean against
Him. Crowd him. Fog out his identity.
Hundreds of hungers mingle with his own,
Hundreds of voices advise so dexterously
He quite considers his reactions his,
Judges he walks most powerfully alone,
That everything is — simply what it is.

(pp. 27, 30)

Not only does the common Black experience relate Satin-Legs to Black people generally, but ironically even his efforts to deny his plainer past make him representative of those Blacks who face the unpleasantness of their environment "in a clear delirium" to seek new identities that are dissociated from their pasts.

One of the most readily dissociated yet most overridingly haunting elements in the heritage of the Blacks is the threat and the receipt of violence at the hands of the whites. As a sobering reminder of the inviolability of place in American society, physical and psychological violence often reach into situations of apparent safety and well-being to wreak insult, grief, and pain on Black people. In literature the impact of such occurrences is heightened when the objects of racial violence are cast in the dual role of family member and victim of society. Hence, part of the poignancy of *Native Son* can be attributed to Bigger's relation to Buddy, Vera, and his mother. The sanctuaries proffered by the families of two of Brooks's Black men, Emmett Till and Rudolph Reed, are overridden by the larger society's compulsion to avenge their transgressions of place.

Beginning with the title "A Bronzeville Mother Loiters in Mississippi. Meanwhile, a Mississippi Mother Burns Bacon," Brooks magnifies the lynching of Emmett Till and its aftermath by capitalizing on the mother-son relationship. The awareness of the Black mother's mere presence heightens the pathos for the reader. She evokes immediate images of the all-too-familiar helpless Black mother whose sons are killed by white men. By juxtaposing the two mothers in the title, Brooks reinforces the effect of the relationship between the Bronzeville mother and her son, Emmett Till. The Mississippi mother burns bacon — she is taking care of a family — but she is distracted by thoughts of the lynching that was done on her behalf. In this way the two mothers, though opposed socially, ideologically, and racially, are ingeniously merged so that the images of the white mother evoke images of the Black mother. George E. Kent is negatively critical of Brooks considering "a White woman, who was the source of the lynching of an early adolescent Black boy, simply as mother." Kent goes on to say, "In doing so, the poet ignores the grotesque historical conditions which the heroine would have to work through before exemplifying the humanity with which she is endowed."[14] The white mother's unintentional yet strong identification with the Black mother, however, is important because it is from the white mother's point of view that the poem is presented. Although distracted also by the necessity to justify the lynching, almost from the beginning the white mother begins to sympathize with the "Dark Villain." This sympathy which continues to grow through the poem, coupled with concern for her own children, leads to the collapse of her world. Her growing hatred for her husband who has been acquitted of the lynching becomes obvious, as it is associated with the awful presence of Emmett Till's mother:

> . . . She wanted to bear it.
> But his mouth would not go away and neither would the
> Decapitated exclamation points in that Other Woman's
>   eyes. (p. 323)

In "The Last Quatrain of the Ballad of Emmett Till," Emmett's mother, like countless Black mothers before her, sits in speechless grief over the loss of her "killed boy."

Family relationships also figure prominently in "The Ballad of Rudolph Reed." The protagonist's "oaken" strength characterizes his role as father. His desire is for a house

> "Where never wife and children need
> Go blinking through the gloom.
> Where every room of many rooms
> Will be full of room." (p. 360)

When Reed finds the one he wants, he applies for it even though it is "in a street of bitter white." After all, Reed is "oakener than others in the nation." Finally, the sight of his youngest daughter's blood sparks Reed to violence. Even at this time, however, he is mindful of his familial obligation. He presses "the hand of his wife" as if to affirm what he must do and to say goodbye.

The strong sense of family that prevails throughout the poem continues after the climax of the action. Small Mabel feels responsible for her father, while her mother pays him the highest tribute by continuing resolutely in the same oaken way that he would have.

To his wife Rudolph Reed is an object of respect and love. While many other men in Brooks's works are presented as love objects, not all of them are positive ones. Men are variously portrayed as disrespectful, coercive, lecherous, weak, and inappreciative of what a Black woman has to offer. In "Queen of the Blues" Mame says they

> . . . are low down
> Dirty and mean.
> Why don't they tip
> Their hats to a queen? (p. 43)

The lines raise the question of how extensively Brooks's female personae see themselves as queens of the blues when they sing explicitly or implicitly about "low down dirty and mean" men.

Certainly "Queen of the Blues" candidly presents Mame's complaints about the disrespect shown by men. The poem, which presents the hard urban life of a female blues singer, is a "blues" within a blues.[15] Both Mame's story and the lyrics of the blues she sings depict the loneliness of a woman. Although the M.C. refers to her as "queen of the blues," the men who pinch her arms and slap her thighs do not respect her.

Closely akin to Mame's complaint about Black men's lack of respect is the observation that selfish coercion is often used by Black men in their relationships with Black women. The persona in "The Battle" is partial to Moe Belle Jackson in her fight with her husband. Obviously a Black woman, the persona implies that Moe Belle Jackson acquiesces too easily and forgives too soon: "And this mornin' it was probably, 'More grits, dear?'" (p. 39).

A similar instance of selfish coercion and disrespect is implied in Chapter 22 of *Maud Martha*, "Tradition and Maud Martha." Maud describes with apparent displeasure Paul's lack of tradition. She particularly contrasts her life with her parents to her life with Paul. She remembers the traditional decoration of the Christmas tree by her brother, sister, parents, and herself. Paul's attention to Christmas, to Maud, and to Paulette their daughter was given in the most perfunctory way. He had argued that he had done his part and that Maud and Paulette would just have to be satisfied with what they had. He had even suggested that if they wanted more, Maud could get a job. These and other arguments appear to have been convenient for justifying his having less-than-refined friends to their apartment on Christmas night and for expecting the disapproving Maud to celebrate Christmas by serving them beer and pretzels. From Maud's point of view, his tone is insensitive and threatening.

Insensitivity to the feelings of women appears as a major trait in men in several other instances. This trait is especially noticeable when it involves the callous desire to use women solely as sex objects. Most often the displeasure of the reproving persona or female character is readily apparent. Such is the case with Mrs. Martin in "When Mrs. Martin's Booker T." While depicting a Black man in an usually strong mother-son relationship, this poem is dominated by Mrs. Martin's feeling of outrage about the mistreatment of women by men. Her outrage is combined with shame in this instance because the man doing the mistreating is her son. It is precisely because her disgust is representative of the feelings of the women around her that she feels such shame. So great is her disgrace that she moved "to the low west side of town." Her son's life is less important to her than the sanctity of a man's proper treatment of a woman. Mrs. Martin's vehemence and the tone of the persona indicate that Booker T.'s "ruining" of Rosa Brown is wanton lechery.

The two men in "Obituary for a Living Lady" are both described as lechers who cause the young woman's pain through their insensitivity and disrespect. The man with whom she falls in love expects her to show her love with sexual favors. When she refuses to comply, he abruptly withdraws his attention. The strong implication is that the man who stopped calling is to blame for her pain and that his interest in her was purely sexual. His turning to "a woman in red" substantiates this idea as the persona cynically faults the man by saying, "My friend spent a hundred weeks or so wishing she were dead."

Even when the woman seeks refuge from her pain in "the country of God," the persona's cynicism persists. The attention that the minister pays to the woman is not seen positively by the persona but rather is imputed entirely to lechery:

> And wonders as his stomach breaks up into fire and
> lights
> How long it will be
> Before he can, with reasonably slight risk of rebuke,
> put his hand on her knee. (p. 19)

Just as Booker T. could find in familial relationships no refuge from the persona and his mother's expectation of the proper treatment of women by men, the preacher in "Obituary for a Living Lady" finds no sanctuary either from expectation of proper treatment or from the suspicion of improper treatment of women by men. Clearly the point of view in some poems is that the lowest common denominator in being low down dirty and mean is simply man.

Such a point of view is less applicable in "The Sundays of Satin-Legs Smith." Although Satin-Legs's main interest in "his lady" each Sunday is sex,[16] there is no hint that he is either insensitive or disrespectful or that "his lady" suffers the least discomfiture by the arrangement. One might even construe this arrangement to be positive except that sex becomes the most important aspect of Satin-Legs's life. The absoluteness of the earth and of sex is reassuring and sustaining to a man who fears the full glare of contrast between the white and Black worlds. Not only does he shun his own past, and fail to recognize it, but he also has no appreciation for "Saint-Saens . . . piquant elusive Grieg . . . Tschaikovsky's wayward eloquence . . . the shapely tender drift of Brahms."

The separateness of cultural worlds, which George E. Kent refers to as "rituals of isolation,"[17] occurs in another instance in "The Sundays of Satin-Legs Smith" that is similar to occurrences among Black men in other poems by Brooks. Although movie-time is often shared by Blacks and whites, their perspectives of the cultural phenomenon remain separate. When Satin-Legs goes to the movies, he exemplifies this separateness and his own relative lack of power. It is the influence of the total Black experience which lends irony to the inability of such a regal peacock even to enjoy *looking* at the white heroine in the movies. His enjoyment of the innocuous frivolity of Mickey Mouse bespeaks his own mouselike impotence. Viewing Mickey Mouse is the one time when the ritual of isolation can be relaxed since Mickey "is for everyone in the house."

"Strong Men, Riding Horses" presents a similar instance of a movie revealing a Black man with a perspective of his own impotence in relation to the white heroes portrayed on the screen. Unlike Satin-Legs, Lester openly compares himself, although unfavorably, to these heroes. Images used to describe the white heroes — strong, desert-eyed, rentless, broad of chest, flailing, saddled, brave — all connote virility, while Lester on the other hand is self-deprecating: "I am not like that. I pay rent, am addled / By illegible landlords, run, if robbers call."

Although a similar sense of inferiority is conveyed by Maud and Paul in Chapter 18 of *Maud Martha*, "We're the Only Colored People Here," it is Paul who feels pressure from Maud concerning his sense of manhood. This instance again involves the movies, where the ritual of isolation if often tested. After the evening begins with Maud's feeling so "precious, protected, delicious" and with Paul's feeling so indulgently chivalrous, the couple self-consciously attend the World Playhouse movie downtown. When Paul observed, "We're the only colored people here," Maud hated him a little. Again when he hesitated to ask the "cold-eyed" blonde girl at the candy counter about buying tickets, "coward," she thought, "she ought to flounce over to the girl herself — show him up." What Maud did not realize was that the pasts of Paul's ancestors leaned against him in the same way that Satin-Legs's pasts leaned against him.

Although Paul and Maud eventually saw and enjoyed the movie and although he said that "we oughta do this more often," she "knew that . . . it would be a year, two years, more, before he would return to the World Playhouse." After all, it is in places such as the movies, where the ritual of isolation is tested, that the glaring insult to the Black people's sense of virility is exposed. Satin-Legs, Lester, and Paul would rather avoid any confrontation between what Kent calls "White expectation and Black reality." Satin-Legs would avoid confrontation by responding solely to the innocuous Mickey Mouse, Lester by completely acquiescing through every demeaning inference to the western's suggestions of his inferiority, and Paul by staying away — not so much from the content of the movie as from the circumambience of the white movie house.

While in varying degrees Satin-Legs, Lester, and Paul have difficulty accepting and valuing the white culture with which they come in contact, by contrast two of Brooks's works, "Second Beau" and "An Encounter," depict Black men actually adopting white middle-class tastes as their own. In some cases this acquisition presents an obstacle to relationships with Black women. In "Priscilla Assails the Sepulchre of Love" and "Bronzeville Man With a Belt in the Back" the estrangement is in the form of a perceived coldness toward and a threat of rejection of the Black woman. In several of Brooks's works the threats become actual rejections of Black women by Black men as they repudiate characteristic Black identity, especially in regard to skin color.

"Second Beau" in *Maud Martha* describes a young man, David McKemster, who recently has adopted white middle class values. He desires to acquire all of the appropriate trappings. He aspires to be "a picture of the English country gentlemen" with the proper dog, pipe, herringbone tweed, haircut, sox, shoes, educated smile, bow, faint imperious nod, and the right books. In his rush to acquire "a good background" like those of the white "chaps" at the university, he is ready to forget his poor and crude background. The relative value he places on the two backgrounds is apparent:

> Whenever he left the Midway, said David McKemster, he was instantly depressed. East of Cottage Grove, people were clearly going somewhere that mattered, not talking unless they had something to say. West of the Midway, they leaned against buildings and their mouths were opening and closing very fast but nothing important was coming out. What did they know about Aristotle? The unhappiness he felt over there was physical. He wanted to throw up. (pp. 170–71)

Maud hears David McKemster say these things, but she remembers that his mother had taken in washing and had said, "I aint stud'n you" and that David himself had had a paper route, washed windows, cleaned basements, sanded furniture, and performed many other odd jobs.

Later in "An Encounter," when Maud sees David McKemster at the university again, she notices how cold he is to her. He acts bored until they meet a young white couple and "David's face lit up." Then he becomes animated. Emulating people of the white middle class has become paramount in his life — he seems to have neither time nor desire to indulge in the company of Black girls.

A similar kind of coldness is presented in "Priscilla Assails the Sepulchre of Love." Priscilla finds it necessary to control her strong impulses carefully toward the male love object in order to avoid the threatened coldness of a rejection. The title suggests a kind of tactical warfare that requires guards upon the heart to protect it from rejection's "winter." This imagery is used similarly in "Bronzeville Man with a Belt in the Back." Here the man is perceived to gird himself in armor to protect himself from exposing his feelings. He appears to be defensive for the same reason that Priscilla says "I can't unlock my eyes." With this armor, however, he can

> Shake off the praises with an airiness.
> And, searching, see love shining in an eye,
> but never smile.
>
> In such an armor he cannot be slain.   (p. 346)

The defensive posture against the threat of rejection in both of these poems is apparently not used by all lovers in Brooks's works. As the title suggests in "For Clarice It Is Terrible Because with This He Takes Away All the Popular Songs and the Moonlights and Still Night Hushes and the Movies with Star-eyed Girls and Simpering Males," Clarice has paid the price for being unguarded against the winter of sorrow brought on by his rejection of her. The man is perceived to be responsible for his change of regard for Clarice and for her consequent change of fortune.

Similarly without such protection for her feelings, Annie in "The Anniad" is also unable to avoid the grief of rejection. Tan man is portrayed as egotistical, opportunistic, weak, confused, frantic, spent, and prodigal, but he wins Annie's love "by easy stages." His pride and egotism become obvious as he quickly adjusts to being worshiped. Soon after the seduction, he leaves for war where his weakness is revealed. When confronted with thoughts of the brevity and tenuousness of life, tan man has a "rummage of desire"; he is baffled when his dissipation leads to impotence. When the war is over, he "wants his power back again." The persona adds here an editorial comment about the nature of men:

> No confection languider
> Before quick-feast quick-famish Men
> Than the candy crowns-that-were.   (p. 87)

Tan man rejects Annie because she is too limpid, too meek to restore his fire. It is significant that skin color, however, is a factor. "Dusted demi-gloom" refers directly to "sweet and chocolate" Annie with the "black and boisterous hair." The importance of color is further emphasized by his description of the kind of woman he seeks. Clearly "gold" is a reference to skin color and the value placed thereon. The description is not only of a licentious woman, but a wicked woman as suggested by the snake images of "hissing" and "coiling." The "gauzes in her gaze" suggest the momentary blotting out of reality. The description of what he gets shows the fulfillment of what he sought: he gets an exotic woman who is in spiritual, mental, and physical contrast to Annie. Tan man's last stages are spent and prodigal. His dissipation with women, liquor, and disease have caused his demise. He returns to Annie to say a final goodbye. The whole experience has left her with new ways of remembering tan man and a new way of forgetting him.

While "The Anniad" includes skin color among the factors affecting tan man's rejection of Annie, several of Brooks's works key solely or almost entirely on skin color as a basis for rejection of Black women by Black men. The implication is readily apparent in the following list of titles: "Stand Off, Daughter of the Dusk," "If You're Light and Have Long Hair," "The Ballad of Chocolate Mabbie," and "Low Yellow." "Helen" and "The Ballad of Pearl May Lee" also involve the rejection of Black women by Black men on the basis of skin color. In the first of these works, "Stand Off, Daughter of the Dusk," the persona suggests that "bronzy lads" will "hurry to cream-yellow shining." A very similar statement appears in *Maud Martha*, "If You're Light and Have Long Hair." Again the title leaves little room for subtlety as Maud summarizes her thought about Paul's feelings for her. She believes that Paul merely tolerates her and that he must "jump over" the wall in order to appreciate her inner qualities:

> But it's my color that makes him mad. I try to shut my eyes to that, but it's no good. What I am inside, what is really me, he likes okay. But he keeps looking at my color, which is like a wall. He has to jump over it in order to meet and touch what I've got for him. He has to jump away up high in order to see it. He gets awful tired of all that jumping. (pp. 213–14)

The "saucily bold" Willie Boone breaks seven-year-old Mabbie's heart in "The Ballad of Chocolate Mabbie" when he rejects her, who "was cut from a chocolate bar," in favor of "a lemon-hued lynx / With sand-waves loving her brow." The pain inflicted by Willie Boone's rejection is basic and devastating. Her black friends are no consolation for her new-found bewildering pain. "Mabbie on Mabbie" indicates that Mabbie is re-evaluating herself and "with hush in the heart" clearly suggests that her self-esteem has suffered. "Helen," Chapter 9 of *Maul Martha*, affords a look at Maud Martha in contrast to her lighter and "more beautiful" sister Helen, who symbolizes light-complexioned Black women or even white women who enjoy favors because of their color. As a child Maud was harshly rejected by Emmanuel in favor of offering Helen a ride in his wagon. The memory of the experience, like Mabbie's, sticks with Maud and haunts other experiences involving lighter women throughout the novel.

"Low Yellow," in *Maud Martha*, shows again Maud's preoccupation with the possibility of Paul's rejecting her because she is dark-complexioned. She is concerned that Paul will think "that any day of the week he can do better than this black girl." Although she seems to be more concerned than Paul about color and its effects on their compatibility, her concern plausibly reflects her experiences of rejection by men on the basis of color.

According to the narrator, Sammy in "The Ballad of Pearl May Lee" gets what he deserved when he is lynched for having sex with a white girl. Sammy's preference for light-complexioned girls is used to justify Pearl May Lee's bitterness. The rejection of a Black woman by a Black man is like a significant number of others in Brooks's works. Not always, however, has the sense of recrimination been as apparent as it is in this poem. The Black man is seen as a bigger villain than either the white girl who seduces and traps him or the mob which lynches him.

As love objects, Sammy and other Black men in Brooks's works suffer in the estimations of the personae and of the Black women in these works when the men disrespect Black women by coerciveness, sex abuse, impotence of character, or rejection of blackness. Understandably, Black men fare more favorably in Brooks's works when they exhibit attractive qualities, however ephemeral, such as devotion and strong and enduring love.

In the light poem, "Patent Leather," "that cool chick down on Calumet" thinks her "brand new cat" is "really 'it.'" In spite of his pitiful muscle and his shrill voice, she likes him and thinks he is man enough for her because of his pretty patent-leather hair. The female persona in the sonnet "Deep Summer" is attracted to the male figure because he is "the headiest of men!" So intoxicating is he that she jests that she needs gloves of ice to wear to neutralize the deep summer effect of his touch. She confesses, however, that she really does not want the gloves or any restraint:

> . . . You gave me this
> Wildness to gulp. Now water is too pale.
> And now I know deep summer is a bliss
> I have no wish for weathering the gale. (p. 119)

Russell in "First Beau" of *Maud Martha* is another impetuous, attractive man who is described by Maud as "a dazzling, long, and sleepily swishing flourish." His boldness, his virility attracts her.

> There he sat before her, in a sleeveless yellow-tan sweater and white,
> open-collared sport shirt, one leg thrust sexily out, fist on that
> hip, brown eyes ablaze, chin thrust up at her entrance as if *it* were
> to give her greeting, devil-like smile making her blink. (p. 167)

The men depicted in the last three works are positive objects of desire that springs unreservedly from their physical attractiveness or boldness of character or both. In several instances, love for a man is expressed through or in spite of circumstances that threaten the attainment of the positive objects of desire. One instance is the threat that war poses for the man in "The Sonnet-Ballad." The persona laments that her lover has been taken off to war and that she knows death will claim him. The poem clearly conveys her love through her apprehension. The passages, "they took my lover's tallness off to war" and "when he went walking grandly out that door," along with her calling him her "sweet love," suggest an attractive man. The lover's importance is emphasized because she is so distraught without him that she has "an empty heart-cup" and wonders "where is happiness?"

Another instance of love for a man being expressed through threatening circumstances is in "The Certainty We Two Shall Meet by God." Here the actual threat is never revealed. Its result, however, is the intrusion of time between the persona and her lover:

> The Certainty we two shall meet by God
> In a wide Parlor, underneath a Light
> Of lights, come Sometime, is no ointment now. (p. 95)

These lines express impatience with the Christian admonition that unpleasant conditions in this world will be replaced by pleasant ones in the next world. This couple wants to enjoy life now and together.

In "Callie Ford" it is not so much the intrusion of time but its own ephemeral nature over which this attraction prevails. Clearly the man is presented as an object of physical desire. In fact, the poem's tension is caused by the contrast between the almost random physical attraction and a more lasting love. The opening lines set the tone of frivolous desire:

> It's a day for running out of town
> With a man whose eyes are brown.

"A man" suggests that no particular lover is referred to but rather that the persona is attracted to men with brown eyes. "Running out of town" itself connotes a spontaneous, perhaps even clandestine, act that gives vent to pent-up desires. Sexual imagery indicates a need to be outside the rigid strictures and order of society:

> We'll go where trees leap up out of hills
> And flowers are not planned.   (p. 359)

Although the man may be the random object of clandestine physical desire, he must proceed in stages to press her hand, discover her waist, taste her mouth. He must call her "very sweet," and she must call him "clever." The next day when the tryst if over, the lovers, chagrined at their headiness, will "hate each other forever."

A similar concern for the transitory nature of love is expressed in "High Up He Hoisted Me." While the poem makes a statement about lovers, it necessarily includes a statement about Black men as lovers. When love is new, it can hallow the crudest of environments. One year later it may have lost its ability to do so. The man in this instance seems to share equally in the unsuccessful attempt to recapture the old magic. It is important to observe that the persona is not accusatory but merely acknowledges with her lover the rapid mellowing of love.

"When I Die" depicts a woman's recognition of and resignation to the transitory nature of love. She presents her husband as a poor man with common simplicity who will do what he has to do. A mutual love is suggested as she says, "he'll lay them on with care" "and wipe his tears away." He is portrayed sympathetically, but she realizes that, through no fault of his own or her own, he will not mourn her long and that some other woman or women will soon take her place. Her ability to say with assurance what he will do and how he will feel is an indication that the two have shared many experiences with each other.

Among the strongest, most positive perceptions of Black men are those as the steadfast lovers of Black women. Indeed, for the most part, it is when these men are almost completely merged with their

women and the emphasis is shifted from first and third person singu-
lar to first and third person plural that the men are most favorably
presented as love objects. These liaisons are characterized by two peo-
ple uniting to form a whole that is greater than the sum of the parts.
The assurance, independence, strength, and defiance derived from
the unions enable the couples to better face the vicissitudes of their
environments.

The environment in the sonnet "A Lovely Love" is exploited by the
lovers with defiance. Their love makes sacred the otherwise negative
qualities of the world around them. Their message is that their love
will flourish regardless of the surroundings:

> Let it be alleys. Let it be a hall
> Whose janitor javelins epithet and thought
> To cheapen hyacinth darkness that we sought
> And played we found, rot, make the petals fall.
> Let it be stairways, and a splintery box
> Where you have thrown me, scraped me with your kiss. . . .

In the octave the terms asociated with the environment are those which
ordinarily would be considered negative: "alleys," "janitor javelins
epithet," "cheapen hyacinth darkness," "rot," "splintery box,"
"scraped." These terms represent the ghetto environment in which
the love must flourish. The sestet helps clarify the ambiguity estab-
lished in the octave through contrast to the nativity:

> That is the birthright of our lovely love
> In swaddling clothes. Not like that Other one.
> Not lit by any fondling star above.
> Not found by any wise men, either.   (p. 347)

"Birthright" refers to the environment that is the necessary inheri-
tance of the Black man's "lovely love." With "swaddling clothes,"
"fondling star," and "wise men," this love suggests that the environ-
ment is the Black man's cross to bear. The lovers choose to disdain
society by enjoying their "birthright" instead of fighting it.

Apparently disdaining the idea that the conventional symbols from
the setting should prompt love-making, the old couple in "The Old-
Marrieds" does not respond to "the pretty-coated birds [that] had
piped so lightly all the day," "the lovers in the little side-streets," "the
morning stories clogged with sweets," and the May midnight. These

symbols and the phrase "quite a time for loving" reflect the conventional notion not only that there is an appropriate time for loving but also that it is an anomaly when the conventional symbols do not prompt behavior associated with loving. George E. Kent comments that the old couple may represent those who "have achieved a condition wherein there is neither a special time for loving nor a need for words, and time for loving is lifelong."[18]

Like "A Lovely Love" and "The Old-Marrieds," "When You Have Forgotten Sunday: The Love Story" depicts a couple rising above their environments to affirm and fulfill their love in their own way. The many experiences the couple has shared in the environment are used to reflect their devotion to each other and the imperviousness of their love against the effects of time. The presumably female persona relates endearment toward memories of experiences with a lover, especially on Sundays, "sitting on the front-room radiator," going "in to Sunday dinner / . . . across the front room floor to the ink-spotted table . . . / To Sunday dinner, which was always chicken and noodles / Or chicken and rice / And salad and rye bread and tea / And chocolate chip cookies," worrying about the threat of war, and going to bed together. In doing so she expresses a certainty that her man will never forget her:

> When you have, I say, forgotten all that,
> Then you may tell,
> Then I may believe
> You have forgotten me well. (p. 21)

Another poem in which an old couple relish their memories together and in which the man is fused with the woman is "The Bean Eaters." Along with their memories, this fusion makes their love unassailable by time and by their shabby environment. Reminiscent of the couple in "When You Have Forgotten Sunday: The Love Story," "dinner is a casual affair." The quality of the pair and, thereby, the quality and strength of the man are apparent. Together they have survived not only with order but with dignity:

> And remembering . . .
> Remembering, with twinklings and twinges,
> as they lean over the beans in their rented back room that
>   is full of beads and receipts and dolls and cloths,
>   tobacco crumbs, vases and fringes. (p. 314)

Even in the face of death "this old yellow pair" are not resourceless because they have each other.

Similarly, in the face of the most hostile of environments the "oaken" love of the Rudolph Reeds can be said even to transcend death. While "The Ballad of Rudolph Reed" is not primarily above love, it is the love between Reed and his wife and family which gives meaning and substance to the poem. Although the verse focuses primarily on Reed, his close identification with his wife is immediately apparent. The third and fourth lines are a testimony not only to the strength of Reed but to the strength of the bond between Reed and his wife. Reed's every concern is for the safety and comfort of his family. The ultimate tribute to their bond of love and understanding occurs when Reed and his wife become aware that he must die and that she must stoically carry on after his death. When he presses the hand of his wife, he is saying goodbye; the couple's mutual awareness of the terms of Reed's death bespeaks the profound love, respect, and pride that they feel for each other. Her support manifests itself in her resolve to persevere.

In Gwendolyn Brooks's view of the Black community's being eclectic, the group necessarily includes the substance of Black people, their trials and their triumphs. While writing from the perspective of a woman, she presents disparate perceptions of the qualities of Black men, especially in their relationship to the larger society and to Black women.

One of the most prominent categories of men includes portraits of the Black man's struggle to achieve freedom and dignity in a racially biased society. In several works the figure is portrayed as a patriot like Dorie Miller and other soldiers, especially in a number of the war sonnets. More often, when the relationship of the Black man to the larger society emerges, he is perceived as social victim.

Sometimes Brooks presents her perceptions of men like portraits without glosses or captions, and at other times she allows the personae to make approving or reproving comments. These comments become part of the pictures themselves and thereby sharpen the focus for the reader. Brooks's pictures of men are well drawn and should be seen, for the most part, as selected details from the larger canvases of her works which capture the Black and ultimately the human condition.

NOTES

1. Arthur P. Davis, "The Black-and-Tan Motif in the Poetry of Gwendolyn Brooks," *CLA Journal*, 6 (Dec. 1962), 90–97, and "Gwendolyn Brooks: Poet of The Unheroic," *CLA Journal*, 7 (Dec. 1963), 114–25.

2. George E. Kent, "The Poetry of Gwendolyn Brooks," Part I, *Black World* (Sept. 1971), 30–43 *passim*; Part II, *Black World* (Oct. 1971), 36–43 *passim*.

3. Beverly Guy-Sheftall, "The Women of Bronzeville," *Sturdy Black Bridges*, ed. Rose Ann P. Bell, Bettye J. Parker, and Beverly Guy-Sheftall (Garden City, N.Y.: Anchor Press/Doubleday, 1979), 157–69.

4. Ibid. 158.

5. W.E.B. Du Bois, *The Souls of Black Folk* (Greenwich, Conn.: Fawcett Publications, 1961), 16–17.

6. Robert W. Mullen, *Blacks in America's Wars* (New York: Monad Press, 1973), 52.

7. John Hope Franklin, *From Slavery to Freedom: A History of Negro Americans*, 4th ed. (New York: Knopf, 1947), 449.

8. Gwendolyn Brooks, *The World of Gwendolyn Brooks* (New York: Harper and Row, 1971), 32. Hereafter, citations from this source will be indicated by page number only.

9. Harry Shaw, *Gwendolyn Brooks* (Boston: Twayne, 1980), 122–23.

10. Northrop Frye, *Anatomy of Criticism* (Princeton: Princeton Univ. Press, 1957), 41–43.

11. Davis, "The Black-and-Tan Motif," 93.

12. Eugene B. Redmond, *Drumvoices* (Garden City, N.Y.: Doubleday, 1976), 280.

13. Ibid., 274.

14. George E. Kent, "Aesthetic Values in the Poetry of Gwendolyn Brooks," in *Black American Literature and Humanism*, ed. R. Baxter Miller (Lexington: Univ. Press of Kentucky, 1981), 90.

15. Shaw, *Gwendolyn Brooks*, 73.

16. Kent, "Aesthetic Values," 88.

17. Ibid., 89.

18. Ibid., 76–77.

R. Baxter Miller

"Define . . . the Whirlwind":
Gwendolyn Brooks' Epic Sign for a Generation

For Mari Evans

For twenty-three years, Gwendolyn Brooks tried to write her epic *In the Mecca* (1968). Her portraits of the Black community began with *Street in Bronzeville* (1945) and continued with *Annie Allen* (1949), *Maud Martha* (1953), and *Bean Eaters* (1960). But these books did not fulfill her ambition to write in the heroic genre. An epic should rank with the classics; it should portray the narrator's journey, the obstacles encountered, and the final vision of victory.

Brooks tried to write a Black epic in the title poem of *Annie Allen* but failed. Because the style was too lofty for the theme, an unintentional mock epic resulted. She had heeded the critics too carefully; their requests had led her to substitute Germanic mythology for the Black folk life that she knew. If Latin and Greek diction replaced the Black vernacular, the folk voice would not be evident.

Before Brooks attempted an epic again, she wrote *Maud Martha*. In this autobiographical novel, she practiced the technique of focusing upon the life of one woman and the characters and problems come upon. Brooks tested, too, her skill for creating an undramatized narrator, the fictional self conceived in the work, who can enter characters' minds or withdraw into objectivity.[1] Her next book, *The Bean Eaters* (1960), continued some good poems, especially those concerning the fifties, yet few of these verses demonstrated majestic finish and thematic depth. The poems did not rival the fine sequences of sonnets that end her first two volumes. Once again she wanted to attempt a long poem. Could free verse and ballad succeed where rhyme royal and sonnet had not? The next book would tell. A year after its publication (1969), George Starvros, an interviewer for *Contemporary Literature,* would question: "Let me ask you about the character in your poetry and in your novel *Maud Martha. In the Mecca,* your most recent volume, portrays life in a large city building. *A Street in Bronzeville* gave similar vignettes of people in the city. The same, I think, can be said of all your work." Brooks replied, "It's a fascination of mine to write about ghetto people there."[2] One can evaluate her success in this effort, first in light of the Anglo-American tradition of poetry, next in the paradox of the American Dream, and finally in some skillful use of techniques such as Christian myth, parody, and narrative distancing. *In the Mecca* is a most complex and intriguing book; it seeks to balance the sordid realities of urban life with an imaginative process of reconciliation and redemption.

Before an explication of the title poem, one needs to know some background. In her interview with Starvros, Brooks comments:

> . . . when I was nineteen and had just gotten out of junior college, I went to the Illinois State Employment service to get a job. They sent me to the Mecca building to a spiritual advisor, and he had a fantastic practice; lucrative. He had us bottling up medicine as well as answering letters. Not real medicine but love charms and stuff like that he called it, and delivered it through the building . . .[3]

Brooks's explanation here closely correlates with the description of Mecca that appears on the back of her title page:

> . . . a great gray hulk of brick, four stories high, topped by an ungainly smokestack, ancient and enormous, filling half of the block north of Thirty-Fourth Street between State and Dearborn . . . the Mecca building is U-shaped. The dirt court-yard is littered with newspapers and tin cans, milk cartons and broken glass. . . . Iron fire escapes run up the building's face and ladders reach from them to the roof. There are four main entrances, two on Dearborn and two on State Street. At each is a gray stone and threshhold and over each is carved "The Mecca." (The Mecca was constructed in 1891, a splendid palace, or showplace of Chicago).[4]

The date of 1891 is significant because it designates the post-Darwinian world. In American history, industrialization had ended the dream of an agrarian world. The Chicago Mecca, in this light, becomes ironic when one considers the other Mecca, the holiest city of Islam and birthplace of Mohammed. Having wanted to write two thousand lines, Brooks settles for slightly more than eight hundred.[5] She says: "This poem will not be a statistical report. I'm interested in a certain detachment, incisiveness. I wish to present a large variety of personalities against a mosaic of clarity, affairs, recognizing that the *grimmest* of these is likely to have a streak or two streaks of sun."[6] The intention is to expand a dramatization of individual scene into universal type so as "to touch every note in the life of this block-long block-wide building would be to capsulize the gist of black humanity in general."[7]

The simple plot and structure of "In the Mecca" (the poem) present an urban setting. For convenience one can divide the narrative into three sections. Part I sets forth the return home from work of Mrs. Sallie Smith, mother of nine. The focus here is on the neighbors that she encounters and on the characterizations of her children. In the second part, the shortest, the woman notices that Pepita, one of her girls, is missing. This prompts the first search through the tenement and allows for further characterization and biblical parody. Part II also concerns the paradox of American myth. The longest section is Part III, which constitutes almost half of the verse. Here the police retrace the Smiths's search. Because of its themes and styles, Part III is probably the richest. The following contribute to its power: militant declarations, interracial lovemakĭng, rhetorical questions, and Christian myth. The poem ends with the discovery of Pepita's corpse under the bed of Jamaican Edward.

"In the Mecca" represents opposite strains of the Anglo-American tradition. One finds a naturalistic version of Walt Whitman, by way of the industrial age, and the redemptive, if frustrated, potential that characterizes the world of T.S. Eliot. But these influences work so that the peculiarities of the Black American experience transform them into a new and creative vision. By adapting to the social forces of the sixties, the poet uses a new milieu. Her canvas is a most demanding time in American history. For this and other times, Gwendolyn Brooks holds to light the soundness of body and mind against the decline of courage and assurance, a lapse which emerged with modernity and the shadow of the holocaust. She continues to believe that imaginative and verbal power challenge and balance finally the danger which posits the insignificance of human life and the indifference to human extinction. For her generation, the defining emblem is ultimately the whirlwind, the collapse of self-confidence, the failure to transform social ill once more into epic victory and to reclaim from the time before the holocaust, and the later accusation of "reverse discrimination" in the United States, the heroic and bluesesque will of Black hope. Whereas for Margaret Walker, cleansing has been the metaphor for the perspective which woman takes on historical and cosmic evil, the depth here every bit as great as Melville's "mystery of iniquity," for Brooks the sign is medication. The artistic process itself plays out the action of healing, while the poem serves as both epic quest and sacramental liberation.

Mary Melodie, one of Mrs. Sallie's daughters, shows this turmoil. She likes "roaches, / and pities the gray rat." To her, headlines are "secondary," even though she knows that "blood runs like a ragged wound through the ancient flesh of the land." The imagery implies the naturalism of Richard Wright and others, for to such writers people are manipulated by forces beyond their control. Yet Brooks's point is not that life is crushed inevitably, it is, rather, that even the most lowly insect is sacred. Such a proposition returns a reader to Emerson's belief that each individual reflects all Being. It leads similarly to Whitman's indebted idea that a leaf of grass indicates Eternal Reality. In her description of Mary Melodie, the narrator disorients the reader.[8] Although the imagery indicates naturalism, the statement suggests transcendentalism. To Mary, the deaths of roaches signify what pervades all Life. The naturalism after 1850 tempers the romantic vision, when the undramatized narrator withdraws from Mary's mind:

> Trapped in his privacy of pain
> the worried rat expires,
> and smashed in the grind of a rapid heel
> last night's roaches lie.

This suggestion of the post-Darwinian universe reinforces the date of 1891 on the copyright page. Similarly it recalls the imagery that helps depict Prophet Williams, an "engine / of candid steel hugging combustibles." Mrs. Sallie describes three of her children — Emmett, Cap, and Casey:

> skin wiped over bones
> for lack of chub and chocolate
> and ice-cream cones,
> for lack of English muffins
> and boysenberry jam.

The ensuing question is a twentieth-century one and could suit well the wasteland: "What shall their redeemer be"? That Brooks' version has a concrete setting in Chicago adds to the intensity of her effect.

The poverty of the three children mentioned above is as real in the second part as in the first. The levels of the narrator's dramatization in verse in the second part move from the particular to the general: personal, racial, urban, and human. By giving a setting of the city, the narrator implies a need for the pastoral, since the human mind conceives by contrasts. It is striking, indeed, to find in her compressed style, resembling that of Pound and Eliot, the truth of Thomas Gray. Still it was this eighteenth-century poet of graveyards who wrote once on the same theme of death concerning the human potential and the genius that can redeem reality.

> And they [the children] are constrained . . .
> upon fright and remorse and their stomachs . . .
> are rags of grit.
>   .   .   .   .
> many flowers start, choke, reach up,
> want help, get it, do not get it,
> rally bloom, or die on the wasting vine.

From the narrator's observation, the plot reverts to a drama of poetry, where Mrs. Sallie still performs the lead. The image and tone suggest both the Old Testament and the folk ballad. "No More Auction Block." In the first part, one finds an emphasis on lost children; in the second, there is an implication of Black death, which is archetypal. The present only foreshadows Pepita's end: "One of my children is gone" (295).

That Don Lee, a poet of the sixties, appears in "In the Mecca" recreates him as a man of its imaginative world as well as a man of history. The Lee in the poem lives at the midpoint between mimesis and reality. He wants "not a various America . . . a new nation / under nothing" (489). One must remember that this Lee is a tenant in the building described, as are all of the other characters. Should the reader elect to jump from the mimetic world to the historical one, he may get into trouble. Like the real Lee (Madhubuti), he may find that only one portrait in the poem is truly distinguished:[9]

> Way-Out Morgan is collecting guns
> in a tiny fourth-floor rooms.
> He is not hungry, even, though skillfully lean.
> He flourishes, ever, on porridge or pat bean
> pudding or wiener soup—fills fearsomely
> on visions of Death to-the-Hordes-of-the White Man.

Madhubuti, of course, has his own followers and his ideology. Here, however, the latter spoils his opportunity to appreciate fully the range of Gwendolyn Brooks. She does depict Morgan with the imagery and power necessary to make him real. But she portrays John Tom, too (no incidental name), St. Julia Jones, and others who have different beliefs. All live in this decaying city; only through imagination can the reader constantly sustain their opposing visions. But in *Mecca* sustenation is all.

The final two hundred lines show once more the influence of Eliot. The refrain, in particular, indicates a sordid world that has profaned what once was sacred: "How many care Pepita?" The prostitutes and harlots are unconcerned, as the phallic imagery shows: "the obscene gruntings / the dull outwittings / the flabby semi-rhythmic shuf-flings." Equally obscene are those people, young or old, who make vulgar love. Preoccupied with their own lives, past and present, the characters lack any answers, and the narrator will have to give her own. These inhabitants of the city can no more acknowledge the sa-credness of procreation than Alfred, the confused poet, can see that divinity is already within him:

> Hush.
> An agitation in the bush.
> Occulded trees.
> Mad life heralding the blue heat of God
> snickers in a corner of the west windowsill.

Other characters inhabit this Mecca, Brooks's wasteland, though they number too many to receive more than passing attention. Among them are Dakara, the reader of *Vogue*; Aunt Tippie and Zombie Bell, who are undramatized; Mr. Kelly, the beggar with long gray hair; Gas Cady, a grave robber; the janitor, a political person; Queenie King, an "old poem silvering in the noise"; and Wallace Williams, proclaimer of his virility. To all, the narrator's answer to the rhetori-cal question applies equally: "these little care, Pepita, what befalls a / nullified saint or forfeiture (or child)."

Set against this background, the description of Alfred becomes particularly significant, for it suggests that the world has passed from hope to hopelessness. For his authorities, Alfred cites Baudelaire, Browning, and Neruda, but his best trick is to parody Whitman. To affirm the redemptive potential of the human spirit, the nineteenth-century poet wrote: "Good-bye and hail! my fancy." To deprive humankind of such belief, Alfred expresses the opposite: *"Farewell, and Hail!* Until farewell again."* Tension separates the literary vision of the past from that of the present.

Other observations show that this is less the world of Thomas Gray and Walt Whitman than that of T.S. Eliot. Consider Aunt Dill, who wears "Tabu" perfume. Little Papa, probably her husband, has been dead for nine years, and all of her children were still-births. As a woman who loves God, she reminds the reader of St. Julia. More importantly, she illustrates the paradox that Pepita faced: to grow into a woman who should be shunned or to die in the innocence of youth. Dill

> Is not
> true-child-of God for are we ever to
> be children? are we never to mature,
> be lovely lovely? be soft Woman
> rounded and darling . . . almost caressable . . .
> and certainly wearing *Tabu* in the name of the Lord.

Usually ambivalent in attitude, Alfred hates Mecca, when he confesses,

> something, something in Mecca
> continues to call! Substanceless
> . . . .
> an essential sanity black and electric
> builds to a reportage and
> redemption
> . . . .
> A material collapse
> that is Construction.

From Alfred, however, one will hardly get the opinion of the undramatized narrator or the implied author. Since the beginning, Brooks has portrayed him as a weak man and an inadequate intellectual. Pepita, on the contrary, is a true poet, just as Alfred is a false one. Despite her youth, she responded to life with sincerity and sensitivity: "'I touch'—she said once—'petals of a rose. / A silky feeling through me goes'" (808–809). For a brief moment the reader receives an alternative vision set against the urban chaos of squalor and hopelessness.

The urban setting reveals the paradox of the American dream. At the beginning, the narrator shifts the focus from her reader to a persona. By combining the imperative and the expository, the verse commences: "Sit where the light corrupts your face. / Mïes Van der Rohe retires from grace. / And the fair fables fall" (1-3). Thomas Earl, one of Mrs. Sallie's children, loves an American folk figure. In tone, however, the narrator questions the validity of John Chapman, now transformed into American legend. She does not mention Mecca, Saudi Arabia, but its reputation for uncultivability suits well the imagery and myth:

> It is hard to be Johnny Appleseed.
> The ground shudders.
> The ground springs up;
> hits you with gnarls and rust,
> derangement and fever, or blare and clerical treasons.

Characterizations in the narrative parody American myth. Melody Mary, Thomas Earl, and Briggs have "gangs rats appleseed." Examine each word within the quotation mark, first as an entity and then as a whole. Each of the first two images implies the urban experience, but the last suggests the frontier. The collectivity of the line leaves the reader with two questions. Is the idea that "gangs" or "rats," as social reality, corrupt myth and dream, "Appleseed," beyond recognition? Or can myth, "Appleseed," redeem the ghetto from "gangs" and "rats"? By their very disjunction such inquiries mislead, for the purpose here is to create not a separation of perspectives but a unity composed of alternative points of view.

One must measure American ideals against the social reality of Mecca. In one scene Emmett, a daughter of Mrs. Sallie, seizes the telephone from John Tom. Considered on various levels of meaning, this incident becomes complex. In a fine wordplay on time and the American Dream, the narrator recreates the folk legend of the submissive Black: "Despite the terror and the derivation, / despite the not *avuncular* frontier, / John Tom, twice forty in 420, claims / Life sits or blazes in this Mecca." When the narrator intervenes, Tom has provoked already the "calm and dalliance" of law. On a second level, the narrator becomes unintentionally ambiguous. An exclamation that concerns the size of Pepita results in the American Dream ironically rendered. The twist is that one can be small in thoughts as well as in dimensions: "How shall the Law allow for *littleness*! / How shall the Law enchief the chapters of / wee brown-black chime, we brown-black chastity." With the arrival of the impersonal policemen begins a second trip through the Mecca, one which ends in the discovery of the dead child. The officers and the character Amos have different ideologies, since the latter is a bitter militant. He says of a personified America: "Bathe her in her beautiful blood."

"In the Mecca," the title poem, portrays the urban scene through a straight or ironic use of Christian myth and through parody. Throughout the plot, the verse changes the point of view between the narrator and her characters. The situation of Briggs, another of Mrs. Sallie's children, reworks a central motif in *Maud Martha*: at some point human concern passes from social reality — a difficult concept with which to deal — to religion and forgetfulness. The narrator first enters into the character's mind and then withdraws. In the initial description of the young man there comes ironic detachment, but after the reader learns about his problems with the gangs in his neighborhood, the vision comes from within: "Immunity is forfeit, love / is luggage, hope is heresy." The narrator, nevertheless, can step back from the character and speak directly; she can explain human psychology brilliantly: "there is a central height in pity / past which man's hand and sympathy cannot go."

Reviewing the first 254 lines of the poem shows that they have described, first, Mrs. Sallie's return home; second, her children; and third, Alfred, the neurotic artist. But line 255 begins the inciting incident, which both the poem and its reader must resolve. Where is Pepita, Sallie's ninth and missing child? The abrupt shift from the narrator's heightened style shocks when Sallie's children reply emphatically in the Black vernacular: "*Ain seen er I ain seen er I ain seen er / Ain seen er I ain seen er I ain seen er.*"[10]

Like most characters in Mecca, Loam Norton worries more about his own concerns than about Mrs. Sallie's daughter. He remembers Belsen and Dachau, the prison camps of World War II, and possibly his own children. But in a parody of the Twenty-third Psalm the narrator interrupts and holds the stage:

> The Lord was their shepherd
> Yet did they want.
> Joyfully, would they have lain in jungles or pastures,
> walked beside waters. Their gaunt
> souls were not restored, their souls were banished.
> . . . .
> Goodness and mercy should follow them
> all the days of their death.

For her character St. Julia Jones, the narrator parodies with equal fidelity the same passage. There the effect was less a religious cynicism than a folk joy. Sallie Smith saw Julia, who asked:

> "Isn't our Lord the greatest to the brim?
> The light of my life. And I lie late
> past the still pastures. And meadows. He's the comfort
> and wine and piccalili for my soul.
> He hunts me up the coffee for my cup.
> Oh how I love that Lord."

When Alfred dreams of being a red bush "In the West Virginia autumn," the image implies the appearance of the Lord to Moses (Exodus 2:3). The narrator knows that man, by being alive, is already divine; Alfred doubts: "the bush does not know that it flames" (511). The force of the ending comes from a repetition of this tone. Jamaican Edward "thrice denies any involvement with Pepita," just as the Peter of the New Testament (St. Matthew 26:4) refuses to acknowledge Christ. The girl lies beneath Edward's cot in the dust. Despite differences in sex and age, she resembles Jesus.

If the title poem, Part I of *In the Mecca*, shows the callousness of the people in the ghetto, Part II, "After Mecca," offers a corrective or redeeming vision.[11] Here Brooks takes historical figures from the sixties and elevates them to a level of myth where they transcend life.[12] First she describes Medgar Evers, the Civil Rights leader assassinated in 1963. Never settling for a mere recording of history, she transforms fact into a tercet of prophecy: "Roaring no rapt arise-ye to the dead, he / leaned across tomorrow. People said that / he was holding clean globes in his hands." In this section, Brooks goes beyond description to symbolism. She reshapes history to make it reflect social vision, created form, and human imagination. Next she portrays Malcolm X, the Black leader slain in 1965. The emphasis, however, should fall not upon history alone but upon Malcolm's role as a political magician. Since the beginning of the volume, such a type of human being has evolved. An artist, like a magician, seeks to create a new order of reality, although the former wants to change the physical world and the latter to institute an imaginative one. By the power of words, the writer seeks to mesmerize her reader with the spell of form. Alfred was a poet, if not a great one; by her life and death, Pepita was more exemplary. The narrator of the verse in "In the Mecca" was, too, for only in her role as seer and harmonizer could she find irony and avoid despair. To envision Malcolm means to reconstruct the many types that precede, as word-maker, ironist, visionary, and prophet:

> in a soft and fundamental hour
> a sorcery devout and vertical
> beguiled the world.
>
> He opened us —
> Who was a key
> who was a man.

At the end of *In the Mecca* redemptive vision depends upon two poems: "The Sermon on the Warpland" and "The Second Sermon on the Warpland" (hereafter "Second Sermon"). The first demonstrates Brooks's ability to portray reality initially from one point of view and then from another, which clarifies the original. The poet reverts to her habit of coining words, as necessary. What does "Warpland" mean? If the word "Sermon" parodies Christ's speech on the Mount, "Warpland" implies not geographical place but military design — a "war planned" — and the problem of distortion, the "warp land." Yet the several strengths, the speakers in the verse, express the opposite yearnings of the human spirit: "Say that our Something is doublepod contains / seeds for the coming hell and health together" (6–7). The voice of a Black militant, shortly afterward, recalls Amos or Way-Out-Morgan in the title poem. But in this world of pervasive irony and contradiction, speech must end in an oxymoron.

> Prepare to meet
> (sisters brothers) the harsh and terrible weather;
> the pains;
> the bruising; the collapse of bestials, idols.
>   . . . .
> the seasoning of the perilously sweet!
> the health, the heralding of the *clear obscure*!   [emphasis mine]

To this voice, Brooks adds a corrective or balancing resonance. Perhaps her greatest gift is a talent for creating opposite viewpoints within the same poetic world. With equal adeptness she can imagine the militant and renew the meaning of Christ's words to His disciple, Peter (St. Matthew 16:18). In both instances she stresses universality within the framework of the Black American experience. To one who has read *In the Mecca* as an objective correlative, the narrator here becomes Pepita, resurrected and grown into womanhood. The figure is older and maternal:

> "Build now your church, my brothers, sisters. Build.
>   . . . .
> Build with lithe love. With love like lion eyes.
> With love like morningrise.
> With love like black, our black —
> luminously indiscreet;
> complete; continuous."

Immediately following this poem, "Second Sermon" results in a final triumph for the human imagination: "This is the urgency Live: / and have your blooming in the noise of the whirlwind" (1–2). The verse has four parts. The first gives the theme quoted last; the second emphasizes the need to give form, to "stylize the flawed utility" (2). In the third division one discovers the chaos against which the imagination conceives. At the end (IV), comes a description of Big Bessie, who stands in the wild weed.

What a metaphor that whirlwind is. From it, one can look at various angles and see diverse personalities, including the arrogantly indifferent, inhumanely callous, and hopelessly contemplative. The narrator's voice reaches back to the end of *Annie Allen*. There, for the first time in Brooks's verse, a speaker possessed some intuitive truth which neither the characters in the poem nor the readers outside fully understood. The observer here is not a well-rounded character; she is, rather, the Imaginative Mind that resolves disparities:

> Not the easy man, who rides above them all,
> not the jumbo brigand,
> not the pet bird of poets, that sweetest sonnet,
> shall straddle the whirlwind.
> Nevertheless, live.

The third and fourth parts show that imaginative vision can save the listeners in the world of Mecca. By perceiving this world, in its contradictions and ironies, the observer has ordered chaos. Is this the final paradox?

> All about are cold places,
> all about are the pushmen, and jeopardy, theft —

all about are the stormers and scramblers but

. . . .

Live and go out
Define and
Medicate the whirlwind.

The noblest virtue of Big Bessie, the woman who concludes the volume, is imagination. Without disillusionment, she can look at life and survive. Brooks owes part of the imagery to Langston Hughes' Semple: "Big Bessie's *feet* hurt like nobody's business / but she stands — bigly — under the unruly scrutiny, stands in the / wild weed (emphasis added, lines 30–32). By vision and endurance, the Big Bessies redeem the city in which the Pepitas are slain.

For twenty-three years, Gwendolyn Brooks had sought this balance of vision. In *Street in Bronzeville*, she had been a poet of the unheroic,[13] but the folk religion lingered. It manifested itself at the end of *Annie Allen* and subsided in *Maud Martha* and *Bean Eaters* only to reappear more intensely in *Mecca*. By then Brooks had practiced ironic detachment and varying distance of narration. Drawing upon Christian myth and different strains of Anglo-American poetry helped her to enrich an epic in which the narrator is heroine. From a certain vision of Chicago as wasteland, Brooks moved to a double perspective of destruction and creation; from Pound and Eliot, her journey led back to Whitman. But the reason is not that Whitman is especially important. It is only that he is romantic in some way that Black folk are: rebelling against constraint, hoping for natural redemption from the depths of an industrial age. If the city corrupts the romantic vision, does it matter? Revealing the paradox of the American Dream suffices, for to show one's reader paradise is not the only way to save his soul.

In the aesthetic formulations, Gwendolyn Brooks remains the talented poet. She imposes the personal voice upon the sources and archetypes of the literary generation. Through the quest for epic form, she combines the impulse toward architectonic space with prophetic invocation, fusing at once the written and the spoken word. Often when she draws upon Judaeo-Christian, historical, and folk sources, through the ornate style or through the vernacular, she opposes the id to the superego, balancing the contradictory tensions which inform human existence. With metaphoric power and intellectual depth, she reconfigures the events of modern history into complex symbol. Whatever her invaluable contributions to the current era, especially from 1945 to 1986, her poetry still signifies two generations past. Yet her language subsumes and transcends historicity.

NOTES

1. See Wayne C. Booth, *The Rhetoric of Fiction* (Chicago: Univ. of Chicago Press, 1961), 149–63, 211–34.

2. Quoted in George E. Kent, "The Poetry of Gwendolyn Brooks," *Black World*, Part I (Sept. 1971), 30–43. Kent writes: "The depth of her responsiveness and her range of poetic resources make her one of the most distinguished poets to appear in America during the 20th century."

3. George Starvros, "Interview with Gwendolyn Brooks," *Contemporary Literature* (March 28, 1969); reprinted in Gwendolyn Brooks *Report from Part One* (Detroit: Broadside Press, 1972), 162.

4. Gwendolyn Brooks, *The World of Gwendolyn Brooks* (New York: Harper and Row, 1971).

5. Gwendolyn Brooks, "Work Proposed for 'In the Mecca,' *Report from Part One*, 189.

6. Ibid., 189.

7. Ibid., 190.

8. Part of my thinking about Brooks as a poet who disorients the reader has its origin in Hortense Spillers, "Gwendolyn the Terrible," seminar paper for the MLA Convention, Dec. 1975.

9. Don L. Lee, "Gwendolyn Brooks: Beyond the Wordmaker — The Making of an African Poet," in Brooks, *Report from Part One*, 22.

10. See George E. Kent, "The Poetry of Gwendolyn Brooks," Part II, *Black World* (Oct. 1971), 36–48, 66–70.

11. To my knowledge, the only article focusing on the volume as a whole is William H. Hansell, "Gwendolyn Brooks' 'In the Mecca': A Rebirth into Blackness," *Negro American Literature Forum*, 8 (Summer 1974), 199–207.

12. To discriminate among myth, romance, and realism, see Northrop Frye, *Anatomy of Criticism* (Princeton: Princeton Univ. Press, 1957).

13. Arthur P. Davis, "Gwendolyn Brooks: Poet of the Unheroic," *CLA Journal*, 7 (Dec. 1962), 114–25. See George E. Kent, "Aesthetic Values in the Poetry of Gwendolyn Brooks," in *Black American Literature and Humanism*, ed. R. Baxter Miller (Lexington: Univ. Press of Kentucky, 1981); R. Baxter Miller, "'Does Man Love Art?': The Humanistic Aesthetic of Gwendolyn Brooks," in *Black American Literature and Humanism*, ed. Miller, 95–112.

Contributors

RICHARD K. BARKSDALE, Professor of English at the University of Illinois at Urbana-Champaign, earned the doctorate at Harvard University. He is editor (with Keneth Kinnamon) of *Black Writers in America: A Comprehensive Anthology* (1972) and author of *Langston Hughes: The Poet and His Critics* (1977). Currently he is composing a monograph concerning antislavery tracts in England. He is the immediate-past-president of the Langston Hughes Society.

FRED FETROW, Chair and Associate Professor of English at the United States Naval Academy, has published articles on Robert Hayden in *CLA Journal* and *Research Studies*. He is author of the Twayne study on Hayden.

R. BAXTER MILLER, Professor of English and Director of the Black Literature Program for the University of Tennessee, Knoxville, earned the Ph.D. at Brown University. He is the author of the *Reference Guide to Langston Hughes and Gwendolyn Brooks* (1978) and has edited, as well as written the final chapter for, *Black American Literature and Humanism* (1981). Having recently completed "For a Moment I Wondered": The Literary Imagination of Langston Hughes," a scholarly monograph for a major university press, he is now finishing a critical and historical study, "The Bullfighter Stands Still: The Writing of Black Chicago from Richard Wright to George E. Kent."

MARIANN B. RUSSELL, Professor of English at Sacred Heart University in Bridgeport, Connecticut, studied on a John Hay Whitney Fellowship and earned the Ph.D. at Columbia University. She has written *Melvin B. Tolson's Harlem Gallery: A Literary Analysis* (1980), which was completed during her tenure on a fellowship from the National Endowment for the Humanities and which won the College Language Association award for distinguished scholarship in 1983.

HARRY B. SHAW, who took the Ph.D. at the University of Illinois at Urbana-Champaign, is Associate Dean of Liberal Arts at the University of Florida and author of *Gwendolyn Brooks* (1980).

ERLENE STETSON, Associate Professor of English at Indiana University, is the editor of *Black Sister: Poetry by Black American Women, 1746–1980* (1981).

JON WOODSON, the published poet and scholar, wrote an acclaimed study on Tolson at Brown University. Having written previously for the *Dictionary of Literary Biography,* he is currently an instructor in business education at the University of Rhode Island.

Index

Black American Poets Between Worlds, 1940–1960 was composed into type on a Compugraphic digital phototypesetter in ten point Times Roman with two points spacing between the lines. Times Roman was also used as display. The book was designed by Jim Billingsley, composed by Metricomp, Inc., printed offset by Thomson-Shore, Inc., and bound by John H. Dekker & Sons. The paper on which the book is printed carries acid-free characteristics and is designed for an effective life of at least three hundred years.

THE UNIVERSITY OF TENNESSEE PRESS: KNOXVILLE

DATE DUE			
MY 19'87			
MY 20'92			